WHY AGILE

WORKS

I0463386

The Values Behind The Results

Michael de la Maza
David Benz

Why Agile Works Mini-book

Published by C4Media, publisher of InfoQ.com.

Production Editor: Ana Ciobotaru
Copy Editor: Lawrence Nyveen
Cover Design: Maiez Mehdi
Interior Design: Dragos Balasoiu

ISBN 978-1-329-91382-0

Contents

Everything Is Agile 1
1.1 Crossing the chasm 4
1.2 Adoption vs. transformation 7
1.3 How the rest of the book is organized 10

Agile Values 11
2.1 Values and beliefs 12
2.2 Values unite, beliefs divide 13
2.3 Organizational culture determines results 16
2.4 Agile is a set of beliefs 21
2.5 The evolution of organizational culture 24
2.6 A quick digression 27
2.7 A values framework for agile transformation 28

Trust 31
3.1 Theories X and Y 32
3.2 Trust equals speed 34
3.3 Aspects of trust 36
3.4 Common organizational beliefs about trust 49
3.5 Example: How to destroy a high-performing team 50

Responsibility 53
4.1 Relationship to trust 54
4.2 Aspects of responsibility 58
4.3 Common organizational beliefs about responsibility 70

Learning 73
5.1 The world is unpredictable 74
5.2 Aspects of learning 77
5.3 Common organizational beliefs about learning 92
5.4 Example: Dedicated learning time 93

Collaboration..95

6.1 Collaboration compared to cooperation 97
6.2 The agile framework for collaboration.............................. 100
6.3 Aspects of collaboration 101
6.4 Common organizational beliefs about collaboration 112
6.5 Example: Collaboration at Pixar... 113

Agile Values Revisited 117

7.1 Culture > process... 118
7.2 If culture > process, why does change focus on process?... 119
7.3 The agile culture and a few recommendations.................. 120
7.4 Coda and kudos 122

Additional Resources 127

References 135

Index..147

PART
ONE

Everything
Is Agile

"In any moment of decision, the best thing you can do is the right thing, the next best thing you can do is the wrong thing, the worst thing you can do is nothing."

— Theodore Roosevelt

The list of companies touting agile is long.

Some of the software companies might be familiar. Spotify is agile. Salesforce is agile. Google, Apple, Amazon, Yahoo, Red Hat, Adobe, and Facebook are agile. Smaller, lesser-known software-development companies such as Atlassian, Paycor, Pivotal Labs, BNA Software, Hotels.com, and DevSpark are agile.

Companies we don't typically think of as agile are working to be agile. Microsoft, a company known for linking releases of their flagship products (Windows and Office) to specific years, claims to be agile. General Electric is agile. Hewlett-Packard is agile. Bank of America is agile. IBM is agile. Key Bank is agile. The BBC and British Telecom are agile. The United States Department of Defense is agile.

The Software Engineering Institute, originator of the Capability Maturity Model (CMM) now known as Capability Maturity Model Integration (CMMI), a top-down approach that is almost antithetical to agile, now claims that it is possible to embrace both [Gla08].

Game developers are agile. Financial companies are agile. Media companies are agile. Banks are agile. Universities are agile.

In *The Agile Mind-Set*, Gil Broza asks an intriguing question: What noun typically follows agile?

Broza writes [Bro15]:

> People talk about agile development, agile project management, agile processes, agile methods, and agile best practices. Some speak about the agile methodology or the agile framework. Others refer to pairings like Scrum/agile and lean/agile.

The language of agile is everywhere.

Consultants talk about becoming agile to avoid disruption. Terms like extreme programming, Scrum, and kanban are tossed around as ways to become agile whether people know what they mean or not. "Sprint", "iteration", "backlog", and "burn down" are all entering the lexicon.

Figure 1.1: Bus-stop advertisement for agile consultants in Chicago.

National Public Radio is agile [Put14].

Forbes describes what agile leaders look like [Dut11]:

> Agile leaders are not only fast and effective problem solvers when dealing with situations they've never dealt with before, but they are also laser-focused on results and excellent at reshaping plans and priorities when faced with unexpected changes in the environment. They are resourceful and competitive. And, they get it done fast.

Offices in Europe being designed for agility include Microsoft Netherlands, Alcatel-Lucent, Unilever Switzerland, W.L. Gore & Associates, and Eneco [Off15]. The European banking giant BNP Paribas is also agile [Sar04]. Singapore's government is investing $1.2 billion in technologies including agile to enhance operational efficiency and public-service delivery.

Agile certifications and assessments abound.

The Scrum Alliance, Scrum.org, the International Consortium for Agile (ICAgile), the Project Management Institute (PMI), LeanKanban University, the Scaled Agile Framework (SAFe), and the Dynamic Systems Development Method (DSDM) consortium all offer agile certifications. The International Software Testing Qualifications Board (ISTQB) and Certified Agile Tester (CAT) offer agile testing certifications. Smaller players such as SCRUMStudy offer niche courses.

Organizations can turn to AgilityHealth, evidence-based management, Comparative Agility, Forrester, SAFe, the Agile Adoption Framework, and the Agile Journey Index (among others) to assess their level of agility.

Sales managers are agile. Training is agile [Gil13]. Librarians are agile [Mck09].

1.1 Crossing the chasm

As agile has spread, the backlash has been fierce.

A number of people have written about the ubiquity of agile and its subsequent loss of meaning. Dave Thomas, one of the original developers of the "Manifesto for Agile Software Development" or Agile Manifesto, has declared [Tho14], "Agile is dead." Thomas suggests that agile "has been subverted to the point where it is effectively meaningless, and what passes for an agile community seems to be largely an arena for consultants and vendors to hawk services and products." He suggests the word has been co-opted to boost sales in the same way that "green" has been used.

Stephen Cohen and Robert Galen have both asked if agile has jumped the shark [Coh11][Gal14]. Tim Ottinger has opined that he wants agile back [Ott14]. The Anti Agile Manifesto has been released as a parody site [Ant15]. Hayim Makabee wrote about the end of agile [Mak14].

A great rant from Tom Elders on *Hacker News* starts with [Eld12] "I can't take this agile crap any longer. It's lunacy. It has all the hallmarks of a religion."

Andy Singleton at Assembla even wrote an article titled "Seven Things I Hate About Agile" to, in his words, "burn off the stink of stagnation" that surrounds the term [Sin12].

What is happening with agile?

According to the most recent "state of agile" survey from InfoQ, agile has gone mainstream and the majority of organizations use agile techniques for at least some software development projects.

We can use Geoffrey Moore's chasm model for technology adoption to get a sense of what's happened in the marketplace with agile. Moore's model for disruptive technologies is useful because it looks at innovations that require people to do things differently — innovations that require behavior changes.

Looking at Moore's model, innovators and early adopters are visionaries with a high willingness for change, high risk tolerance, and strong support from management. Early adopters understand the benefits and are willing to experiment in order to gain a competitive edge.

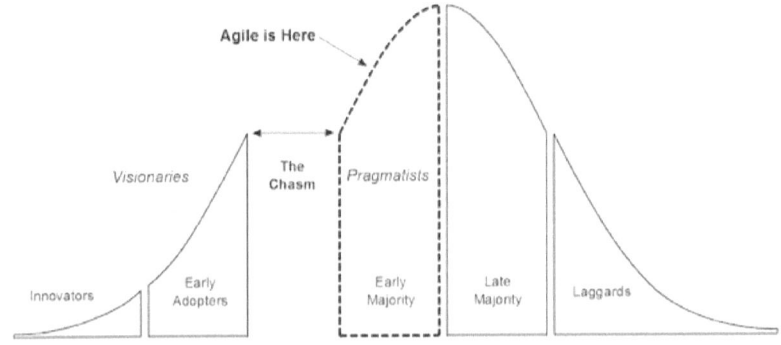

Figure 1.2: Geoffrey Moore's model for crossing the chasm.

There is a large gap or chasm between these innovators and early adopters and the largest segments of the market: the early and late majorities.

Pragmatists and conservatives on the other side of the chasm are far more likely to approach agile from a completely different perspective. They are risk averse. They have heard of agile but likely think it is a process change that they can easily roll out to their IT organizations. Their risk tolerance is low, they want quick results, and they're expecting relatively easy-to-implement process changes.

In other words, they are driven by practicality and want an out-of-the-box solution. The early majority wants technologies that are simple to implement.

As a result, many vendors and consultants have figured out that they can take advantage of the industry buzz and the early majority's desire for practicality to sell agile tools and processes to convince these customers they are becoming more agile. As William Pietri wrote on the Agile Focus weblog [pie11], "An idea that provides strong benefits to early adopters gets watered down to near uselessness by mainstream consumers and too-accommodating vendors."

Much of this has happened in the agile marketplace as early adopters sought out-of-the-box tools and processes.

Coaches and consultants with experience in making the transition are spread thin and many new consulting organizations look to take advantage of the situation and sell their services.

The early majority also sees agile as a process to enhance productivity rather than a potentially disruptive culture change. Agile can (depending on existing culture) be a significant cultural change. Crossing the chasm is more difficult with agile than with other innovative technologies because organizations might not have a culture that is ready for agile and either don't understand or underestimate the cultural change inherent in agile.

The Agile Manifesto reads:

We are uncovering better ways of developing software by doing it and helping others do it.

Through this work we have come to value:

- Individuals and interactions over processes and tools
- Working software over comprehensive documentation
- Customer collaboration over contract negotiation
- Responding to change over following a plan

That is, while there is value in the items on the right, we value the items on the left more.

The Agile Manifesto describes a change in beliefs, a cultural change.

Tobias Mayer described it this way in *The People's Scrum:*

> Scrum is a framework for organizational change and personal freedom. It is not a methodology, it is not a process, and it is much more than a tool.

Agile is a set of beliefs, a set of ideas. Are executives and leaders willing to adopt and champion these ideas? Or are they merely looking to "optimize" employees because employees are seen as the constraining element of the system?

If you look at agile-consulting organizations, how many of them are process, tool, or methodology heavy? How many of them want to sell a system for doing agile?

As Dave Thomas writes [Tho14]:

> Now look at the consultants and vendors who say they'll get you started with "Agile." Ask yourself where they are positioned on the left-right axis. My guess is that you'll find them process and tool heavy, with many suggested work products (consultant speak for documents to keep managers happy) and considerably more planning than the contents of a whiteboard and some sticky notes.

Moore's ideas about crossing the chasm help us understand that what is happening is normal for innovations that impact behavior.

We don't believe agile is dying or jumping the shark, but rather is experiencing growing pains as it reaches new markets. In many cases, however, what this means to organizations on the other side of the chasm is that what they're doing or attempting to do is not really agile.

1.2 Adoption vs. transformation

One of the more common mistakes made when implementing agile is not seeing it as a framework for organizational change. This typically looks like adopting sprints and the artifacts associated with sprints and ignoring other components of the change framework, most often agile values.

When asked why agile projects fail, the number two reason cited in VersionOne's 2014 "State of Agile Survey" after "None of our projects failed" was "Company philosophy or culture at odds with core agile values."

Henrik Kniberg tells the story of one of his most successful projects — a system built for the Swedish police that allowed them to use laptops in the field — and what happened afterwards [Kni13]. Because the project was extremely urgent, the group was allowed to use an agile approach and break out of the traditional organizational culture. Everything went well, the police organization viewed it as a success, and the project even won a "project of the year" award.

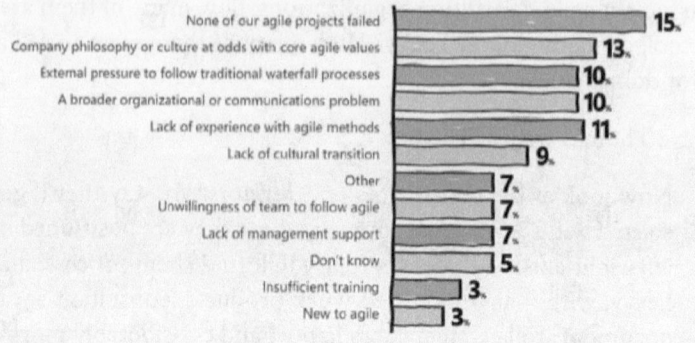

Figure 1.3: From VersionOne's 2014 "State of Agile Survey".

What came next, however, was even more interesting. A high-level decision was made to rebuild from scratch that same system police had used in the field, using Siebel. This was part of a standardization effort to reduce the complexity and number of systems. Not only was the decision made to use a technology that the development team didn't agree with, but it was decided to use a more traditional, sequential project-management approach to development. Development took a couple years and when it finally rolled out, it was a disaster because the police found it to be slow and clumsy and basically unusable. Making the change even more difficult was that the police preferred their existing system, which worked. Kniberg estimates that this cost the Swedish police more than £1 billion.

Adopting agile practices is likely to lead to marginal improvements at best if current values and culture are out of alignment with agile beliefs and the organization doesn't change.

Similarly, when asked about barriers to further adoption, inability to change organizational values was cited as the top barrier in VersionOne's 2014 survey.

As Mike Cottmeyer wrote in "Untangling Adoption and Transformation" [Cot11]:

- Transformation is about changing the "agile being" side of the equation.
- Adoption is about changing the "agile doing" side of the equation.

Some symptoms that might indicate that transformation has not yet fully happened and agile culture and values have not yet been adopted are:

- Agile teams have defined dates and scopes.
- A manager assigns tasks to team members.
- Impediments to development are not addressed.
- Team members don't point out problems when they see them.
- Testing is not allowed because it highlights shortcomings.
- Burn-down charts are altered to present a rosy picture.
- Management plans rather than teams.
- All features are seen as high priority.
- Communication is one way, from leaders to employees through broadcasts.
- Agile is seen as something "the technology people do".
- Teams are not developing working software.
- Teams are reporting rather than discussing progress.
- Superstars are valued over team.
- No changes affect how things are done.
- There is a reluctance to hire qualified outside experts.
- Leadership demands results without providing direction.
- Knowledge is hoarded.

To realize the full benefits of agile requires the values or the "being" part of agile.

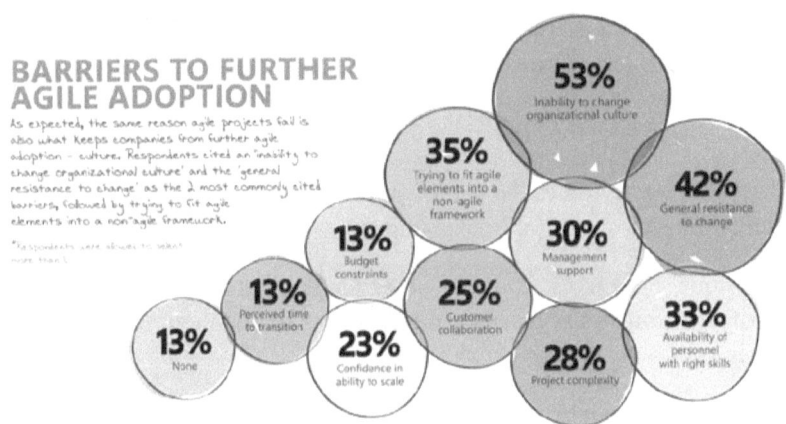

Figure 1.4 Barriers to agile adoption, from VersionOne's 2014 "State of Agile Survey".

Michael Sahota and others have discussed how agile processes and methods can be adapted to different cultures [Sah04]. We would like to take a different approach. We believe that if organizations adopt agile as a set of beliefs, they will develop an agile culture and that this agile culture is what leads to continuous adaptation and innovation. The focus of the change effort must be on the heart, not the head or the hands.

Processes and methods can become stale and rote, and can stifle innovation — even processes that were initially developed to be agile. An agile culture, however, will continuously improve and adapt without the need for periodic change initiatives.

Numerous books and best practices exist to help organizations with implementing agile practices, or the "doing" side of the equation. Our reason for writing this book is to examine the values and culture that make organizations agile.

1.3 How the rest of the book is organized

Chapter 2, "Agile Values", describes the difference between values and beliefs, discusses why organizations should care about culture, outlines the results pyramid and Fredric Laloux's model of organizational values, and introduces a simple framework for agile values.

Chapters 3 to 6 discuss the four major components of the agile values framework (trust, responsibility, learning, and collaboration), use examples to show what these look like in agile organizations, and highlight differences in how they are often interpreted.

Chapter 7, "Agile Values Revisited", summarizes key learnings and recommendations for organizational change.

"Additional Resources" contains other materials that can help with agile transformation and key charts and questions to ask about organizational values.

Chapters 3 to 6 can be read in any order.

PART
TWO

Agile Values

"I believe that we all have the potential to solve problems and express ourselves creatively. What stands in our way are these hidden barriers — the misconceptions and assumptions that impede us without our knowing it."

— Ed Catmull, *Creativity, Inc.* [Mic15]

2.1 Values and beliefs

To explore organizational culture and how it influences performance, we'd like to start by looking at individual values and beliefs — not specific values or beliefs, but rather what these terms mean.

People associate values with character. We associate values with ethics. We associate values with who we are. Someone who has values is someone to look up to, someone that is like you or that you want to be like, someone who lives his or her life in a certain way.

In *On Value and Values*, Douglas K. Smith writes [Smi04]:

Values are nouns, but nouns concerned with verbs of attitude and action. Values sort into several categories. People refer to social values and political values; and, to family and religious, and environmental values. Values are estimations not of worth but of worthwhileness. Unlike value, talk of values ignores money; it opines on timeless appraisals instead of transient ones. There is a deep backward- and forward-looking quality to values. If value is what makes us wealthy, values, we assume and regularly assert, are what makes us human.

Examples of values include:

- honesty,
- loyalty,
- learning,
- trust,
- family, and
- leadership.

A belief, by way of comparison, is something we hold to be true.

Both values and beliefs guide our actions and behavior. Because they seem so similar, the difference between the two can be confusing.

Beliefs come from our experiences with our families, our culture, our communities, our education, and our jobs. Examples of beliefs include:

- If you want people to treat you well, treat them well.
- Knowledge is power.
- The world is made up of idiots and we're two of them.
- People make decisions based on facts.

If beliefs are things we hold true, values are what we believe are important. The connection between the two is that beliefs influence values and how we prioritize values.

For example, someone who believes that knowledge is the key to a better life is probably going to place a high value on education. If we believe predicting the future is impossible, we tend to value experimentation over planning.

Similarly, we can think of organizations as having values and beliefs. Instead of individual values and beliefs, which differ from person to person, these are the shared values and beliefs that determine how an organization performs.

2.2 Values unite, beliefs divide

An important distinction between values and beliefs is that values unite people while beliefs tend to divide people. This is because people tend to have a similar set of values even though they may be prioritized differently. For example, it's hard to argue that collaboration is important. However, if you made a true/false statement of belief like "Collaboration is more important than safety," some people would agree and some disagree depending on their own experiences. Asserting something is true or most important can be a point of contention because people tend to feel passionate about what they've learned through their experiences.

Think about how hard it is to get a group of people to unite around different religious beliefs or different political beliefs or different cultural beliefs. They will fight morning, noon, and night defending their beliefs.

Yet if you ask them how they feel about "family" or "freedom" — values that everyone holds in some way, shape, or form — you tend to find wide support. Thomas Jefferson, for example, united people by finding a shared value of people of faith: freedom of religion. Jefferson wrote the Virginia Statute for Religious Freedom [Act86]:

> Be it enacted by the General Assembly, that no man shall be compelled to frequent or support any religious worship, place, or ministry whatsoever, nor shall be enforced, restrained, molested, or burthened in his body or goods, nor shall otherwise suffer on account of his religious opinions or belief; but that all men shall be free to profess, and by argument to maintain, their opinion in matters of religion, and that the same shall in no wise diminish, enlarge, or affect their civil capacities.

Jefferson's statute became the basis for the First Amendment of the U.S. Constitution. This work was one of only three accomplishments he instructed be put in his epitaph.

Here's an exercise you can conduct to demonstrate the difference between values and beliefs. This exercise can be done with two or more people. You will need Post-it notes for everyone involved. To practice, you might want to first try it with one other person.

1. Take five minutes and write down as many of your values as you can think of, one to a Post-It note. Don't worry if you can't think of everything. This is not a competitive exercise. It's a collaborative exercise. If at any point during the collaboration, you think of something you forgot to write down, you can add it.

2. Look at what you've both written down and combine all of the values that are the same.

3. Look at what you've each written down that might be different, but that you agree is a value you also hold. Add all of these Post-its to the combined list of values. These are the values you share. Don't dwell on any Post-its that are not in common.

4. Things to think about:

5. How similar or different are your values?

6. Were any of the values listed statements of truth or beliefs?

Figure 2.1 is an example of values shared by two people who have very different backgrounds.

Figure 2.1: Combined values exercise.

In this example, duplicates included:

- family
- friends/friendship
- relationships/trust/"I've got your back" kinds of relationships
- love
- helping others/activism/commitment to the good of others
- "a higher calling"/purpose
- equality/all "men" created equal

Other values that both participants agreed upon included:

- generosity
- kindness
- honesty
- faith
- peace
- fun

- faithfulness
- freedom
- responsibility
- good health
- work
- life
- government "of the people, for the people, and by the people"
- education
- leadership/strength

The result of this exercise is a powerful visualization of shared values. While the participants might have disagreed on specific beliefs due to their different backgrounds and experiences, their overall values were very similar.

In Jefferson's day, to get different religions that believed different things to unite as a country, it was necessary to find values that they all held in common. One such value was freedom of religion: everyone should be free to practice their religion so long as beliefs didn't interfere with other people's freedom.

This distinction between values and beliefs is important to highlight as we begin to consider organizations because individuals will have different values and beliefs and these values and beliefs may be quite different from an organization's. This difference is perfectly normal. However, it's important to note because, more often than not, it's discussions about beliefs that cause friction. If you want to find points of commonality, it is easier to start from values than beliefs.

2.3 Organizational culture determines results

In *Change the Culture, Change the Game*, Roger Connors and Tom Smith describe organizational culture as an organization's experiences and beliefs.

They then visualize the relationship between beliefs and results using a results pyramid. In this model, experiences foster beliefs, beliefs influence actions, and actions produce results.

Figure 2.2: Roger Connors and Tom Smith's results pyramid.

In this model, it's the culture (experiences and beliefs) that really produces results. They describe it this way:

> Culture depends on results; results depend on culture. Leaders can build a company culture around any set of desired results: market dominance, sales growth, technological excellence, ease of customer interaction, best-in-class quality, or stable earnings, just to name a few. Once you clearly define the targets, then you must move quickly to build a culture that produces the right experiences, beliefs, and actions to achieve those results.

The authors used a pyramid instead of a simple hierarchy to highlight the fact that culture plays a much bigger role in determining results than actions do because actions depend on culture. Culture determines how and what employees do in a given situation.

A classic mistake that organizations often make when trying to improve performance is to focus only on the top of the pyramid. Organizations often change processes (actions) while ignoring the fact there are reasons why people think and act the way they do. This disconnect can cause significant issues if the processes are out of alignment with the core culture.

If the organization only focuses on actions and new actions go against organizational culture, process changes are unlikely to last or have meaningful impact.

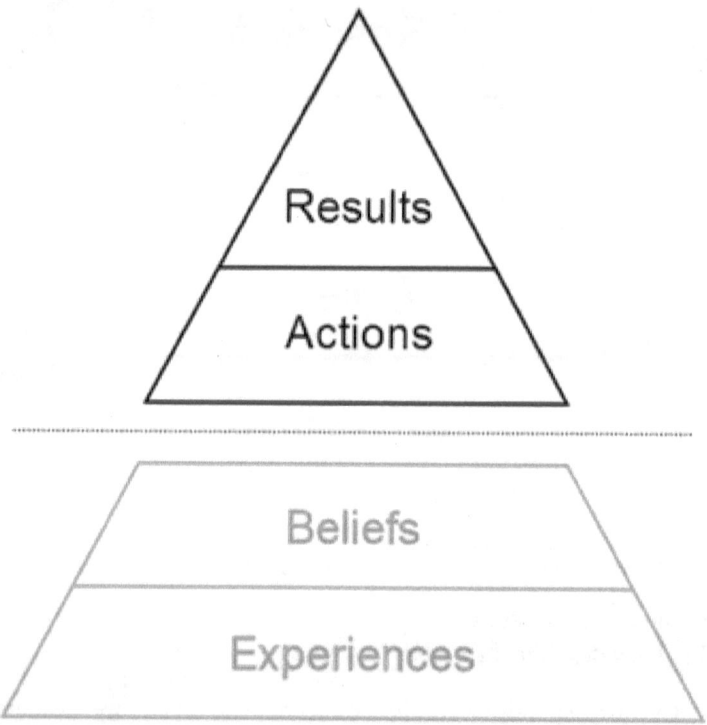

Figure 2.3: Often, organizations focus on the top.

A great example is a hospital that wanted to improve the speed of its surgical-tray sterilization procedures. Without talking to the people who sterilized the instruments, management ordered several million-dollar robotic tray systems. Had they talked to the people in the sterilization department, they would have learned that the real problem was declining morale because the staff viewed new managers as micromanagers. Instead of solving the problem, the decision only reinforced the organizational view that employees were not to be trusted. The new robotic tray dispensers also greatly slowed the process because each could only dispense one tray at a time; previously, multiple employees could retrieve surgical instrument trays.

The hospital could have avoided millions of dollars in process and technology changes and increased speed had management been able to recognize the cultural issues and simply asked and involved employees. The micromanagement culture led to millions of dollars of waste.

To truly transform an organization requires working with the pyramid's full depth and breadth.

In *The Culture Game*, Dan Mezick expands beliefs into beliefs, values, and principles. In Mezick's version of the results pyramid, similar to individual values and beliefs discussed above, organizational beliefs inform values and their prioritization. Beliefs inform organizational values and people develop principles or heuristics based on these values.

Experience, beliefs, values, and principles form the organizational culture that determines actions and results.

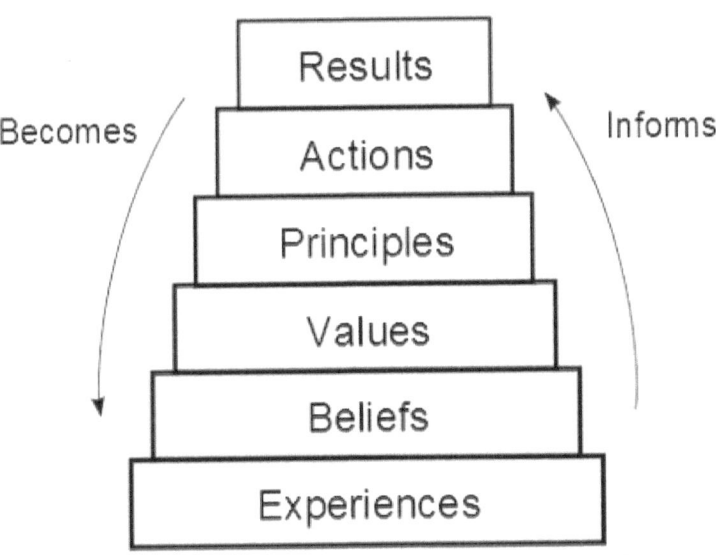

Figure 2.4: Mezick's version adds values/principles and the feedback relationship.

Mezick also depicts the feedback loop of the relationships. Results are not simply a one-way relationship but rather a feedback loop that is constantly building as results become organizational experience.

An organization that tries something new and gets good results might revisit some of its beliefs so that these new beliefs become part of the culture. This process is organizational learning.

Adding values and principles is critical to highlight because as beliefs change how we prioritize, our values change. As beliefs change, priorities change. This, in turn, influences principles (or rules of thumb) and guides our actions and results.

Expanding beliefs into beliefs, values, and principles tells us more about organizational culture and how it works and evolves.

Often, some of the organization's values and beliefs are written down in a mission or values statement. A few examples include:

- "Create fun and a little weirdness" and "Deliver WOW Through Service" — Zappos [Zap15].

- "Trust and personal responsibility in all relationships" — IBM [IBM15].

- "Build the best product, cause no unnecessary harm, use business to inspire, and implement solutions to the environmental crisis" — Patagonia [Pat15].

- "Don't be evil" — Google's former slogan, which they dropped in 2009 [For09].

- "Inspiring humanity" —jetBlue [Jet15].

- "Offer the customer the best possible service, selection, quality, and value" — Nordstrom [Nor15].

It's just as easy, however, to find mission statements that don't represent the actual organizational culture. One of the more famous recent examples is the culture at British Petroleum and the Deepwater Horizon oil spill.

In 2009, part of BP's mission statement read [Ama13] "We aim for no accidents, no harm to people, and no harm to the environment."

From the *Final Report on the Investigation of the Macondo Well Blowout* [Dhs11]:

> Analysis of the available evidence indicates that when given the opportunity to save time and money — and make money — tradeoffs were made for the certain thing — production — because there were perceived to be no downsides associated with the uncertain

thing — failure caused by the lack of sufficient protection. Thus, as a result of a cascade of deeply flawed failure and signal analysis, decision-making, communication, and organizational-managerial processes, safety was compromised to the point that the blowout occurred with catastrophic effects.

The report cited BP's corporate culture as the reason for the Deepwater Horizon oil spill. They claimed to have a culture of safety. In reality, however, the culture was about deadlines and cutting corners to make money.

More often, the difference between written culture and the unwritten culture isn't quite as extreme. One example is a company that promotes teamwork while evaluating and rewarding based on individual performance. Another common example is companies where employees work 12-hour to 16-hour days while the company promotes itself as having a healthy work/life balance.

Organizational culture is the set of shared experiences, beliefs, values, and principles — both stated and unstated [Dun14] — that determines results.

2.4 Agile is a set of beliefs

Agile is a set of beliefs and principles, a set of statements that a group of people proposed to be true from their experience about complex software development.

Again, the Agile Manifesto states [Fow01]:

> We are uncovering better ways of developing software by doing it and helping others do it. Through this work we have come to value:

- Individuals and interactions over processes and tools
- Working software over comprehensive documentation
- Customer collaboration over contract negotiation
- Responding to change over following a plan

> That is, while there is value in the items on the right, we value the items on the left more.

These statements are broad belief statements about what should be valued. These four statements compare two organizational worlds. A world that values individuals over processes and tools is going to look very different from a world that values processes and tools over individuals. The latter world views organizations as machines and the ultimate goal is to find the the perfect set of processes to make the machine run smoothly. This world believes that an organization is like a machine and people within the organization are like cogs or parts that can be optimized.

Valuing individuals and interactions defines a very different organizational world. In this world, an organization is more like a family. When we think of families, we don't typically think about defining processes that everyone in the family needs to follow. We don't think about maximizing productivity by implementing new management routines for each family member. We tend to think more in terms of how each member of the family can realize full potential.

Just this one statement about individuals and interactions shifts how we think.

While most people try to understand the processes in their approach to agile, we would like to take a different approach and outline what this world looks like from a cultural standpoint.

The four main Agile Manifesto beliefs are high-level beliefs that focus on prioritizing values. The Manifesto also includes 12 agile principles, heuristics, or best practices about how to best develop working software:

1. Our highest priority is to satisfy the customer through early and continuous delivery of valuable software.

2. Welcome changing requirements, even late in development. Agile processes harness change for the customer's competitive advantage.

3. Deliver working software frequently, from a couple of weeks to a couple of months, with a preference to the shorter timescale.

4. Business people and developers must work together daily throughout the project.

5. Build projects around motivated individuals. Give them the environment and support they need, and trust them to get the job done.

6. The most efficient and effective method of conveying information to and within a development team is face-to-face conversation.

7. Working software is the primary measure of progress.

8. Agile processes promote sustainable development. The sponsors, developers, and users should be able to maintain a constant pace indefinitely.

9. Continuous attention to technical excellence and good design enhances agility.

10. Simplicity — the art of maximizing the amount of work not done — is essential.

11. The best architectures, requirements, and designs emerge from self-organizing teams.

12. At regular intervals, the team reflects on how to become more effective, then tunes and adjusts its behavior accordingly.

These principles are best practices for development compared with the four higher-level value-ordering beliefs.

As Dan Mezick described in his results pyramid, principles are more like heuristics that, in this case, guide software development, while beliefs are higher-level statements of truth. For example, the fifth principle elaborates on the meaning of valuing individuals and interactions over processes and tools. It provides specifics on how to successfully complete projects: give people the environment and support they need and trust them to get the job done.

Principles follow from values follow from beliefs.

If beliefs influence values and values inform principles, as we've seen, one of the natural questions that arises is what do the organizational values look like in an agile culture? How does adopting agile beliefs affect an organization's values? What does a culture that values individuals and interactions over process and tools look like?

If we view agile as a philosophy or a set of beliefs, implementing agile might well lead to organizational change beyond adopting a set of processes or methods. It might well lead to a desirable change in organizational culture and values.

When groups adopt agile beliefs, the adoption process might change or influence the culture depending on the organization's existing culture. Or the culture may influence agile adoption. As we've seen, organizational culture is the primary reason cited for failures in agile transformation.

This point is also critical to understand because many people still see agile differently. They see it as a process or methodology. They see agile as something that affects actions, not necessarily as a framework for change. They don't see it as a set of beliefs with the potential to change their culture.

If an organization is approaching agile from a process or methodology perspective, it is not likely to get the desired results. Similarly, if the existing values in an organization are far from alignment with agile values, the effort is likely to either fail or be significantly greater than anticipated.

2.5 The evolution of organizational culture

Fredric Laloux, in his book *Reinventing Organizations*, outlines a history of organizational cultures [Lal14] as part of his goal to create better organizations. Through his research and that of others, he discovered that organizations tend to evolve in stages. All models and research strongly converge on and support this stages theory.

Laloux describes the stages with colors ranging from magenta to teal with everything before magenta represented by the invisible-to-the-eye infrared, a stage where the only communal relations were basically familial.

Figure 2.5 illustrates this evolution of organizations along a historical timeline.

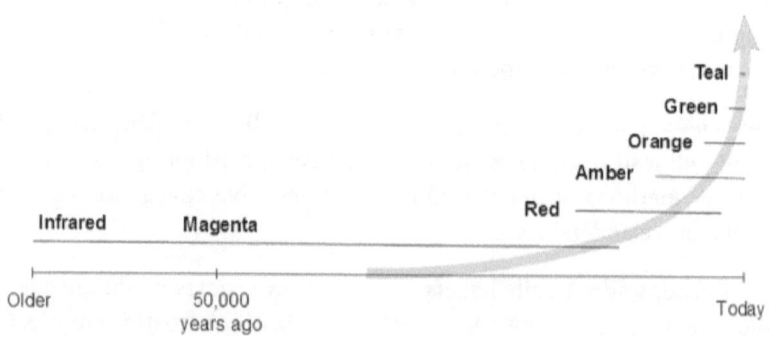

Figure 2.5: Laloux's evolution of organizations.

Laloux's model includes the challenges that confront organizations and the innovations that lead to subsequent breakthroughs towards the next stage. In addition, he describes the characteristics of the culture and many of their values.

The model provides a way to look at organizational development by looking at the history of how different types of organizations evolved, the challenges they faced, and how they innovated to adapt to these challenges. The model also provides a way to look at some of the different value priorities in each of the different stages.

Table 2.1 lists the characteristics and breakthroughs of each stage.

Organization	Breakthroughs	Characteristics
Red (wolf pack, mafia)	• Division of labor • • Command authority	Strong, tough, dangerous, power, armies, street gangs, mafia, force
Amber (army)	• Long-term perspective and processes • Size and stability (formal hierarchies)	Static, fear, right or wrong, institutions, bureaucracies, castes, social classes, order, predictability, roles, guilt, compliance, army, hierarchy, processes, certainty
Orange (machine)	• Innovation • Accountability • Meritocracy	Achievement, empirical, science, expertise, truth, entrepreneurship, modern, innovation, materialistic, accountability, meritocracy, rationality, performance
Green (family)	• Values-driven culture and inspirational purpose • Empowerment and multiple stakeholder • Perspective	Feelings, fairness, equality, postmodern, harmony, community, cooperation, consensus, relationships, service, values-driven, purpose

Teal (living system)	• Self-organizing • All breakthroughs of previous stages	Trust, collaboration, service, pride, networks, learning, self-organizing, wholeness, community, fun, purpose, power, teams, facilitators/coaches, ownership, responsibility, resilience, compassion

Table 2.1: Characteristics of organizations (red to teal).

Primitive groups in the infrared stage were largely familial and subsisted largely on foraging. At this level, there is little division of labor and therefore almost no organizational model. The concept of self is virtually indistinguishable from others.

The magenta level is the tribal level. At this stage, groups shift from small family units to groups of up to 100 people. Authority figures, such as elders and shaman, arise but there is little organization beyond that.

Most of the organizations we're familiar with are red through green organizations.

In developed societies, red organizations typically exist on the fringes of legality. They look like street gangs or mafias — non-trusting, tough, dangerous, and forceful. Amber organizations are still commonly found among government agencies, the military, public schools systems, and religious organizations. Orange organizations are dominant in the corporate and business world. Green organizations are common in non-profits and have also been making inroads in the business world. Ben & Jerry's and Patagonia are a couple examples of businesses that fit well within green paradigm.

Teal organizations, which Laloux sees as emerging, are still uncommon.

In terms of Laloux's model, agile requires a green or teal organizational culture for transformation. It could also be said that agile beliefs define a teal culture that, if not realized, undermines successful transformation. Organizations that have the most success with agile are either at the green/teal stages or are moving towards the green/teal stages.

From our experience, what Laloux describes as a teal culture and what we've seen of agile cultures are very similar.

Our goal is to specifically bring to the surface and outline with examples the values of agile organizations to make them clear and easier to understand. For instance, collaboration means something very different in a teal organization than in an orange organization.

Describing the values of agile organizations not only helps transitional organizations understand whether they are moving in the correct direction but it also helps organizations spot cultural conflicts that might prevent agility.

2.6 A quick digression

Before discussing values of an agile culture, we'd like to address a question that tends to come up in any discussion of values.

Bluntly, the question is "Is one set of values better than another?"

No. Laloux does not advocate one organizational model over another, but rather he looks at how and when organizational paradigms map well to different situations. Similarly, we see our efforts as a way to look at agile organizations and talk about how these organizations define themselves through their values and how these values influence decisions.

Second, we'd like to make a clear distinction between organizational values and individual values. As Laloux states [Lal14]:

> I'm referring to systems and culture, not people. If we look at an organization's structures, its practices, its cultural elements, we can generally discern what worldview they stem from.

At any moment in time, different people act on different values and principles depending on their situation. People tend to switch back and forth quite easily between norms depending on the group they are interacting with.

Here, we are talking about the values of organizations and, in particular, what organizational values are required for agile transformation.

2.7 A values framework for agile transformation

Agile is more than a tool to achieve better results. Agile is a framework for organizational change that leads to a more human-centered organization.

We have discussed beliefs and values, and how agile is a set of beliefs. But what do these beliefs lead to? What does an agile organizational culture look like?

To come up with a simple framework for agile values, we drew on our own experiences with teal, green, orange, and amber organizations and a set of criteria for considering values and their relationship to the Agile Manifesto.

The criteria for our framework is as follows:

- Are the values consistent with our experience and the experience of others in agile organizations?
- Do the organizational values follow from Agile Manifesto beliefs or do they support any of the Agile Manifesto's 12 principles?
- Is our value list simple and useful?
- For our purposes, simple means simple enough to be easily committed to memory so that the list is easy to mindfully practice with the ultimate goal of guiding behavior, decisions, and actions.
- Completeness may be sacrificed for the sake of simplicity if simple covers almost or near enough values.
- Useful means does it help people understand what the core organizational culture should look like to support agile transformation?
- If we removed a value from the organizational culture, would it be significantly less useful? In other words, would it seriously impact agile transformation?

Using these criteria, we came up with the four values in Figure 2.6.

Aspects of these values are similar to the five values the Scrum Alliance defines: focus, courage, openness, commitment, and respect.

When we looked at existing models of agile organizational values and applied the criteria above, we found current models incomplete. Many contained pieces or parts of the whole, but nothing presented a full picture.

For example, the Scrum Alliance values don't specifically mention learning as an organizational value. Jeff Sutherland and others, however, have discussed the importance of rapid iterative learning and retrospectives [Sut14].

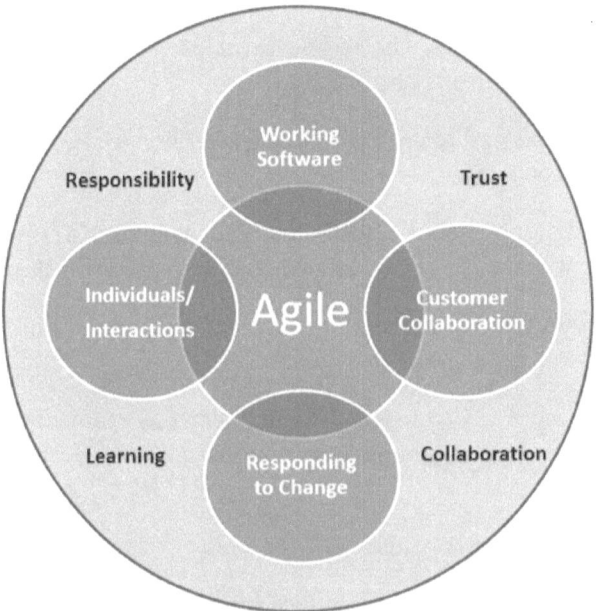

FIgure 2.6: Agile values framework.

Each of these four values — responsibility, trust, learning, and collaboration — has several aspects that are critical for agile transformation. A short list of these is shown in Table 2.2.

Trust	Responsibility	Learning	Collaboration
Openness	Autonomy/ Freedom	Risk	Transparency
Credibility/ Integrity	Motivation	Feedback	Self-organization
Craftsmanship	Commitment	Adaptability	Communication
Empathy/ Respect	Mutual Responsibility	Sharing	Unity/ Shared Purpose

Table 2.2: Aspects of agile values.

We found it helpful to pull together a single broader picture.

Throughout this chapter, we've highlighted reasons for putting together this cultural model of agile values. Here, it helps to summarize the reasons:

1. Agile is crossing the chasm and experiencing growing pains with more conservative organizations.

2. Many people and many of these organizations see agile as a process or a methodology.

3. Organizations should understand that agile is a framework for change when they are deciding whether to pursue transformation.

4. Agile adoption (doing) is very different from agile transformation (being).

5. Cultural conflicts are cited as the number-one reason agile projects fail and inability to change organizational culture is the top barrier to agile adoption.

6. Culture determines results.

7. An understanding of agile culture can help executives make better decisions about agile.

8. Much literature has been written about implementing Scrum and XP and kanban and relatively little has been written about agile culture.

9. A better understanding of the destination might improve the journey.

In subsequent chapters, we'll dive deeper into the model and share examples where appropriate to paint a picture of agile culture and talk about some of the differences among amber, orange, and green cultures. The goal is not to provide a comprehensive picture but to provide a useful picture.

What do these values look like, what are some of the beliefs that might undermine them, and what beliefs can we introduce and model to lead to successful agile transformations?

PART
THREE

Trust

"The best way to find out if you can trust someone is to trust them."

— Ernest Hemingway

3.1 Theories X and Y

An interesting question to ask people is whether they believe people 1) are lazy and tend to avoid work, or 2) are ambitious and self-motivated.

It's a great question because it makes people think. When you ask it, most people tend to lean one way or the other and after a minute or so of thinking about it say, "It depends."

"It depends" usually means it depends on the person.

Douglas McGregor, in his book *The Human Side of Enterprise*, proposed that a manager's assumptions or beliefs about human nature determined a management style [Mcg60].

McGregor developed two theories of management, Theory X management and Theory Y management. Theory X leaders assume that people:

- dislike and will try to avoid work whenever possible;
- are lazy and prefer to be directed;
- are not creative or natural problem solvers; and
- must be coerced, controlled, directed, or threatened with punishment to get them to put forth sufficient effort.

Theory X leaders tend to take either a hard or soft approach to motivation. The hard approach is command and control: coercion, implicit threats, micromanagement, and tight controls. In two organizations that have been models for command and control, the army and the church, authority has been enforced through punishment such as court martial in the army or excommunication in the church.

The soft approach is to motivate through money in exchange for cooperation. The hard approach results in hostility and purposely low performance. The soft approach results in increasing demand for rewards in exchange for diminishing work output.

Abraham Maslow's hierarchy of needs is a way to think about individual growth as progressing upward as different needs are met or satisfied [Mas43]. At the bottom of the pyramid are physical needs, such as food, sleep, and water, and safety needs, such as protection and health.

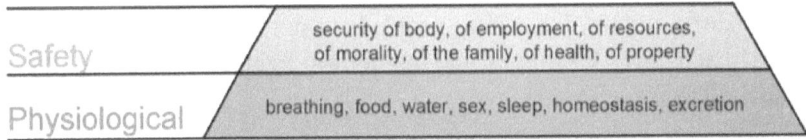

Figure 3.1: Maslow's physiological and safety needs.

Both Maslow and McGregor argue that when a need is satisfied, motivation lags or disappears. In modern society, needs at the bottom of Maslow's hierarchy are in many ways satisfied and might no longer provide sufficient motivation. When dependence is complete, as in a parent/child relationship, the "because I said so" model will work for a while. As people progress upwards in Maslow's hierarchy, however, authority no longer has the same effectiveness and reliance on authority might encourage countermeasures and lower performance.

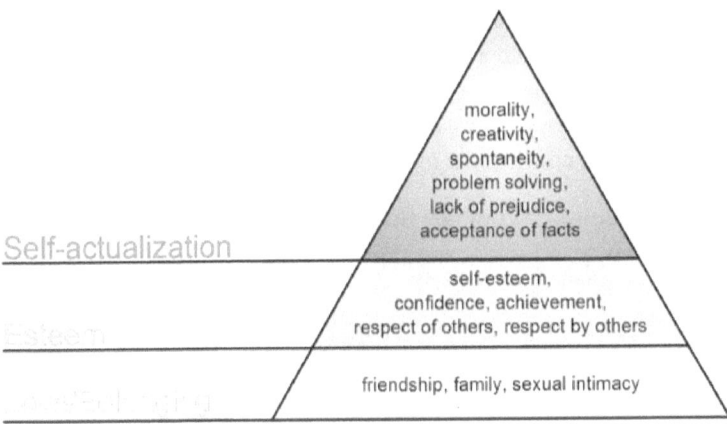

Figure 3.2: The top of Maslow's hierarchy of needs.

Theory Y management is based on the top of Maslow's hierarchy of needs and focuses more on what individuals want to achieve for themselves.

Theory Y leaders believe:

- Work can be fun and a source of satisfaction.
- People are motivated and self-directed in the service of objectives to which they are committed.

- People learn not only to accept but also to seek responsibility.
- People are creative and natural problem solvers.
- Motivation occurs by looking for ways to match an individual's personal needs with organizational needs.

McGregor recognized that some people have not reached the level of maturity that Theory Y assumes, and might need tighter controls until individuals develop.

Theory Y suggests that organizations will be more effective if they acknowledge and accommodate their employees' needs and goals. Modern organizations can do this with flexible hours, retirement programs, health care, onsite fitness centers, dedicated time and budget for training and self-improvement, and maternity leave. Theory Y managers tend to be more hands off. They allow employees a great deal of freedom to achieve results. These managers recognize individual needs for autonomy and let employees manage themselves. Theory Y managers often involve employees in decision making as well.

One point to note here is that results tend to reinforce assumptions. That is, if a manager holds Theory Y's assumptions and establishes working relationships within which individuals are trusted and encouraged to do what they do best, people will be more motivated and self-directed. If managers hold Theory X's assumptions and micromanage people, the outcome will tend to confirm the manager's suspicion that people are lazy.

The reality is often more complex than this, but this feedback loop provides a valuable way to look at assumptions and their impact on organizations.

At the heart of McGregor's Theory Y is trust in individuals.

3.2 Trust equals speed

People often think about trust as a "touchy feely" to have far down the priority list in our age of business, hard data, numbers, and reasoning.

Stephen M.R. Covey, son of Stephen R. Covey of *The Seven Habits of Highly Effective People* fame, uses these two simple formulas to make the business case for prioritizing trust [Cov06]:

- $\downarrow$ Trust = $\downarrow$ Speed + $\uparrow$ Cost

- ↑ Trust = ↑ Speed + ↓ Cost

As trust increases, speed increases and cost decreases.

A great example of these simple formulas is the regulations passed in response to the Enron, Tyco International, and WorldCom scandals. These companies and others were cooking the books and when investors found out, it led to a collapse in their share prices, which cost investors billions and shook confidence in the entire U.S. stock market.

The subsequent laws passed restored trust in the system but this trust came at a cost. The cost is compliance and record keeping associated with Sarbanes-Oxley. Our point is not to argue in favor or against the act but merely to demonstrate that if there were a way to increase trust between companies and the public without this act, speed would go increase and cost would drop.

You can think about this in your own relationships at work.

- How much faster is it to get help from colleagues if you know them and have a trusted relationship?
- How much easier is it to ask people you know well for help?
- When you don't know someone or have a trusted relationship, what do you have to rely on?

Often working with people who are located far away, we sometimes use virtual teams. The most critical thing we learned with virtual teams was that we need a significant amount of time (at least a week) to kick off a project in person.

At kickoffs, it is important to lay out goals, prioritize actions, and figure out an initial commitment plan. The most important thing, however, is to build working relationships with the people on the virtual project team. We learned we could get away with not planning everything. Project plans can always be adjusted if you work with people you trust.

Failing to establish trusted relationships, however, is a completely different animal. Failing to develop trust early will almost always lead to complications. This point might seem obvious, but think about how much time people typically spend on planning and how much they spend on building relationships at the beginning of projects.

For reasons like these, agile specifically values individuals and interactions over processes and tools. Trust is also established through these agile principles:

- Face-to-face communication — the most efficient and effective method of conveying information to and within a development team is face-to-face conversation.

- Trust between business people and developers who "must work together daily throughout the project".

These principles help build relationships and levels of trust. With a virtual team, trust is even more important. Why? Because it's harder to have the higher-touch interactions that agile specifies as critical.

Does this mean it's not possible to follow agile with virtual teams? No. What it takes, however, is a significant level of trust and strong relationships. This reality is why we always prioritized at least a week for face-to-face meetings and relationship building with virtual team projects.

One of the reasons virtual teams are often discouraged in agile is because it is so much easier to build trust and strong relationships in a face-to-face setting. When teams work in proximity and trust each other, they have an almost instant understanding of where everyone is and what everyone is doing and they can immediately deal with any issues that arise.

These agile principles help build relationships and levels of trust.

3.3 Aspects of trust

Briefly, Table 3.1 illustrates some high-level aspects and signs of trust in organizations and their importance to agile.

Aspects of Trust	Importance to Agile
Openness	Openness is necessary for continuous improvement. If something isn't working or could be improved, maybe there's a better way. If people can communicate the difficult, issues can be addressed.
Credibility/ Integrity	Credibility enables business people and developers to work together daily. Integrity leads to credibility.

| Craftsmanship | Craftsmanship is one of the first ways people involved in a shared project learn to trust each other, through delivery in small increments. |
| Empathy/Respect | Respect and empathy allow people to understand each other. This is part of valuing individuals and interactions over processes and tools. |

Table 3.1: Aspects of trust.

The next four sections look more closely at these aspects of trust.

3.3.1 Openness

Trust increases when motives are straightforward and based on mutual benefit.

- Do you hear the bad as well as the good?
- Are issues raised or hidden?
- Do people understand why things are done? How transparent are decisions?

In an agile culture, it's important to be honest in order to delight customers. If issues are raised early, you can address them. Also, sometimes what you hear are symptoms rather than actual issues. It might take a little digging to get to the issue and this occurs much more quickly if you can have honest conversations.

Michael on the difference between openness and honesty

To me, there is a difference between openness and honesty. The difference is similar to the difference between answering a question and answering the intent behind a question.

Here's a short example to clarify. I was the lead coach in an engagement and was responsible for bringing in other agile coaches. During the process, coaches wanted to know how long the engagement would last. Obviously, this information would help them plan their lives.

I was working for a consulting company, whose official answer was, "The client would like you to be here for a year."

Now, I had data on coaches who had worked with this particular client, which showed that 70% of coaches left within six months for a variety of reasons.

An honest answer to the question would be to simply repeat the official line from the consulting company about how the client was looking for coaches for a year. An open answer to the question, however, is to say, "The client would like you to be here for at least a year. However, 70% of coaches leave within six months."

The open answer might lead to follow-up questions such as "Why do coaches typically leave within six months?" Typically, people want to know the length of an engagement because they need to make calculations about their lives. Providing them with the facts helps them decide.

Open answers often lead to difficult conversations and this is a good thing.

David on how openness leads to addressing issues

As an instructional designer, I was once asked to improve the strategic quarterly review meeting for the learning organization. The executives wanted to improve the meetings and make them more engaging so they asked our group if we could use technology to achieve that.

My director called me and said, "We've been asked to use technology to improve the quarterly review meetings."

I laughed.

"Why are you laughing?" my director asked.

"Because I don't think any amount of technology is going to fix that meeting," I said.

Having been to past meetings, I knew the issue wasn't a lack of technology. The issue was that the meeting took an entire day and the format was boring. Each presenter was given an hour and each felt obligated to use the entire hour so it was a series of roughly eight hour-long presentations. No amount of technology was going to fix this problem.

After a quick discussion, my director agreed with me. This open conversation, in turn, allowed me to ask, "Is technology really the right solution for making the meeting better?" We agreed that it wasn't. The meetings needed to be shorter and more focused.

We decided to run the meeting in a pecha-kucha format. In this style, each presenter must use 20 slides for 20 seconds each, for a total of presentation time of 6:40 minutes.

Figure 3.3: People gathered for a pecha-kucha presentation.

To tell a story in this fashion, you have to keep your message short and you have to think about how to tell it visually. Allowing 20 minutes for questions and discussion after each presentation, we still cut the meeting to four hours with a 15-minute break at the two-hour mark.

It was a bit of a risk because we didn't know how pecha-kucha would be received. We also had to overcome some pushback from presenters who swore they could never tell their stories in 6:40.

But the executives loved the meeting. They had 20 minutes after each presentation to ask questions and this allowed them to get what they wanted. At the end of the meeting, the executives commended the practice. Our chief learning officer even talked about using the technique in other meetings.

Because I had a trusting relationship with my director and our group encouraged the freedom to question, we were able to talk about and discover the issue and then come up with a simple solution that exceeded customer expectations.

3.3.2 Integrity and credibility

Trust relies on credibility. If people see leaders in the organization say one thing and do another, it undermines credibility. Without actions to back them up, value statements are just words.

In *Software for Your Head*, Jim and Michele McCarthy refer to this quality as integrity [McC02]. Their simple definition of integrity is the unity of thought, word, and deed:

> Although that definition may seem abstract, personal integrity is itself an abstract thing. Integrity can be presumed when someone does what he has previously promised to do, or behaves as if he believed in what was said previously. If your actions and words align consistently, you will be judged by others to have integrity. For all practical purposes, if you act as if you have integrity, then you do have integrity.

Most employees can quickly tell you what to believe about their company's mission statement. Often, there are some distinct differences between what the company claims to stand for and the actual culture.

Enron was the extreme example of a company with no integrity. Enron's stated values in its mission statement were respect, integrity, communication, and excellence [Ant15]. Here is how the company defined respect:

> We treat others as we would like to be treated ourselves. We do not tolerate abusive or disrespectful treatment. Ruthlessness, callousness, and arrogance don't belong here.

The fact that ruthlessness, callousness, and arrogance are even mentioned should have been a warning sign. As corporate communications editor James Kunen wrote [Kun02], "I've read hundreds of companies' vision and values statements, and nowhere have I seen a single reference to ruthlessness, callousness or arrogance — let alone all three."

Integrity leads to credibility.

Integrity and credibility are also big issues in the branding world. Brands stand for something and if you deliver on this promise, you can be hugely successful. If, however, what you stand for and what you're delivering are two different things, credibility can be an issue:

- Do actions match words?
- Do incentives match rhetoric?

- Are people rewarded for actions that demonstrate values?

In an agile environment, credibility helps business people and developers coordinate. The faster both sides can establish that they mean what they say, the more trust they build, and they can quickly work together to deliver value.

David on the importance of credibility to training and sales

In 1998, Cisco Systems moved into the world of IP telephony with the purchase of Selsius Systems. By 2004, IP telephony was becoming more than just phone calls over an IP network. The vision was absorbing all communication over the Internet: voice, video, and data. The network could be used as the platform for what would become known as "unified communications" (UC). [For05].

Early sales for IP telephony were built on a strong return on investment (ROI) related to bypassing traditional long-distance call charges. As the technology evolved into a more complete communications platform, the sale changed. The benefits of UC became softer benefits related to how customers might do business differently.

For example, time to market for perishable goods is critical in the transportation industry. If drivers find that they can't reach a destination, shipments must be redirected immediately or lose value. Therefore, drivers need the ability to instantly reach key decision makers who can redirect shipments to alternative destinations. Another example is simply the ability to easily set up WebEx meetings for employees at different locations with different schedules.

If sales teams understood what was most important to customers and how customers currently used communications, they could talk about how UC and collaboration technologies could improve business. This sale is a consultative sell that we also referred to as business transformation. Because the customer sale was no longer based as much on cost saving, our training group was asked to create a business-transformation workshop for sales teams.

Part of the challenge was that this type of a sale, a consultative sale, was quite different from how sales teams had been selling IP telephony. To sell IP telephony, account managers could previously simply pitch return on investment from toll savings to telecom managers. Consultative sales often involved learning more about the business and talking to people outside of the telecom and IT world.

As we put together the workshop and talked with sales teams that had conducted successful business-transformation engagements, one thing became clear: a consultative sales cycle took longer than a technical sales cycle.

Why did this matter?

Because everything sales teams did revolved around weekly commit calls. Account managers had commit goals and they were asked weekly for progress updates. Every person we talked to said that consultative sales were at odds with the commit calls. We risked contradicting ourselves. Management seemed to be saying, "Take more time for a consultative sale," yet incentives and bonuses were based on weekly commits.

While building the workshop and talking to sales teams, we were advised that we would struggle to convince the sales force if we were to advocate longer sales cycles without eliminating or somehow addressing the weekly commit calls.

We had a couple of ideas for how to resolve the conflict, but as a team we decided we needed to raise the issue to sales leaders. One, we weren't sure if they fully knew what they were asking and, two, we decided we needed executive backing for our proposals or we knew we'd face fierce opposition.

We reached out to one of the sales vice presidents and told him we did not want to send a mixed message to Cisco sales teams. The vice president said the weekly commit calls weren't going away anytime soon. We then pitched our idea that account teams selectively target one to two customers for consultative sales. Larger teams that focused on a single enterprise customer wouldn't have an issue but mid-market account managers could selectively target one to two customers for a longer sales cycle. More time might be invested up front, but there was potential for much larger sales down the road.

The vice president agreed this sounded reasonable and agreed to support the workshop.

In retrospect, we realized the importance of working upfront with account teams. They told us what worked and what issues we might face. As a result, we were able to have an honest conversation with executives and raise issues we'd encountered in order to resolve them in a credible way.

The sales force highly rated the subsequent workshop and business transformation became part of the sales process that continues to this day in Cisco's collaboration group [Cis15].

3.3.3 Craftsmanship

Early agile adoptions focused on empowering people, reducing bureaucracy, improving visibility and collaboration, and adapting to changing requirements. Early agile adoption assumed craftsmanship and that if teams could refocus on getting the bureaucracy out of the way, craftsmanship would shine through.

In reality, some teams lost the focus on technical excellence. As Sandro Mancuso writes in *The Software Craftsman* [Man15]:

> Simply adopting Scrum, having daily stand-up meetings, and having tools to manage backlogs and work in progress won't magically improve the quality of the software or make developers better. Improving the process without improving technical excellence is pointless.

This was never the intent of agile, and for this reason, we state craftsmanship explicitly as an aspect of trust so that technical excellence and development skill remain front and center in the agile culture. In any type of complex development environment, whether it's engineering, software, hardware, instructional design, or architectural design, trust is often based on demonstrated skill and quality.

Scientific management has its roots in the industrial revolution and the writings of Frederick Taylor. Taylor believed that people were like interchangeable parts of a machine. He believed the best way to run a company was to have each person doing a job in an exact, prescribed manner so that the company would function like a watch or a mechanical engine. Taylor's model is the assembly line.

How well does this model adapt to complex development? Not very well. Complex development is a creative process and trying to design and develop in assembly-line fashion puts the focus on the process and not the goal of delivering value to the customer. There is also not necessarily one best way to design and develop. Different software developers, for example, could easily come up with different code that does the same thing. Different architects might come up with different building designs that meet a customer's need.

For these reasons, people like Bill Pyritz at Lucent recommend a crafts-manship model for complex development [Pyr03]. Think about any complex development as similar to learning a trade skill like blacksmithing or violin making: developers progress from apprentice to journeymen to craftsmen to master craftsmen.

Figure 3.4: Civil War blacksmith illustration in Harper's Weekly, 1863.

While we don't advocate for these specific roles, we believe that there is benefit to having more senior and skilled members of a team coach more junior members.

Pyritz writes:

For craft teams to work, a commitment is required from management, the craftsmen, and the other members of the team. Most importantly, each team member must truly love his/her work and be skilled in the craft.

Both customers and internal coworkers look for signs of quality and craftsmanship.

Stephen M.R. Covey, in *The Speed of Trust*, writes that we judge competence (or craftsmanship) based on capabilities and results. Capabilities are our talents, our skills, and our knowledge. Results are our accomplishments [Cov06].

If you were interviewing a software developer with a terrific history of coding experience for a management position, you would ask about management capabilities. Similarly, if a person lists only skills, you would wonder what the person has accomplished with those skills. As teams grow and work together, more senior members should look for opportunities to coach junior members and junior members should reach out if there are areas of expertise in which they would like to improve and develop as craftsmen.

Customers look for craftsmanship in organizations to trust that they will receive value:

- What is the organization's definition of quality? Is it different internally than with customers?
- Does the organization meet or exceed customer expectations?
- Does the branding and marketing match the delivery? Does the organization do what it promises (and more)?
- How do coworkers learn about each other's skills and results within the organization?
- What's the relationship between sales and delivery?

By encouraging delivery of small increments, the philosophy of agile can help demonstrate craftsmanship, both within teams and to customers.

3.3.4 Empathy and respect

Empathy and respect are both critical to trust and have a great deal in common. Respect is one of the key feelings people tend to want from others and empathy is the ability to put yourself in another's shoes.

Agile organizations tend to be flat organizations due to the belief that the best designs come from self-organizing teams. One way to consider a self-organizing team is that it has no authority implicitly derived from structures. A better way to reflect on it is that everyone on a self-organizing team has authority.

In this type of environment, respect does not come from hierarchical position but from skill and from showing respect to others. You receive respect when you show respect for others regardless of how they treat you.

In terms of communication, respect often means listening, acknowledging, and discussing rather than attempting to force your own viewpoint. When people don't feel respected, they often respond with anger or blame. Conflict naturally results from differing ideas and different opinions but can be mutually resolved and often leads to better conclusions when there is respect from all sides.

Empathy is the ability to understand other people — not to necessarily agree with them, but to understand them.

U.S. Army Lieutenant General William "Gus" Pagonis, in charge of logistics during the 1991 Gulf War, said [Tur05], "No one is a leader who can't put himself or herself in the other person's shoes."

Empathy is seeing yourself in another person's situation. The focus is on connectedness, on partnership, and on both of you coming together to accomplish a shared goal. When you can empathize with other people and understand their perspectives, it is much easier to have respect for them.

In agile organizations, empathy and respect help people value individuals and interactions over processes and tools.

Some questions to ask about empathy and respect in organizations are:

- How is respect observed in the organization? What examples of respect and empathy can you cite?
- How are differences viewed in the organization?
- Are people more inwardly focused or outwardly focused? Do they tend to think about others or their own self-preservation?
- What characteristics are respected within the organization?

David on the waiter rule

We invited a team in India new to our learning group at Cisco Systems to dinner at our hotel restaurant. New team members from all over Bangalore met us there.

When I came downstairs from my hotel room, I realized that there were seven restaurants at this particular hotel. I had no idea which restaurant we were meeting at and had to ask. I thought the new team members might be confused as well, so I waited at the hotel entrance to let people know where we were as they were coming in.

We had an excellent meal, enjoyed meeting everyone in a more personal setting, and the onboarding sessions went quite well with everyone engaged in the discussions and activities we'd planned.

Months later, after becoming friends with one of the new team members, I asked about the team's experience and perceptions of the training in Bangalore.

He told me that one of the things they talked about for days was how I had met them at the front door and directed them to where everyone was meeting. He said it made them feel really comfortable and valued, especially as new team members. He told me quite honestly that there was a perception of Americans as self-focused, a perception which I had challenged simply by thinking of them.

I had no idea until months later that the entire team of new hires had discussed this small action and was something they remembered from the training. I hadn't thought twice about it until it was brought up.

Later, I found out that what I'd experienced was an example of the waiter rule: how you treat those in positions of lesser power or authority says more about your character than how you treat those in positions of greater power or authority.

In other words, everyone is going to treat the CEO with respect. Doing so says nothing about your character. What's telling is how you treat others that don't hold any authority over you. Interestingly enough, many CEOs tell similar stories about learning the lesson of the waiter rule [Jon06].

Figure 3.5: The waiter rule. Reprinted with permission. [Mor06]

3.4 Common organizational beliefs about trust

Most people hold similar values. Where they tend to differ is in how they prioritize these values. Their prioritization tends to come from their experiences, their background, their culture, or their religion. Their beliefs, what they hold to be true, influence the importance they attach to different values.

If they've had positive experiences trusting people, they will tend to prioritize trust. If they've had negative experiences, they may rank command and control higher.

Because beliefs and experiences shape values, here are some other beliefs that you want to emphasize and work towards in organizations to build trust:

- People are reliable, self-motivated adults capable of making important decisions.
- People are responsible for their decisions and actions.
- When they understand a goal, people will find the best way to work towards that goal.
- People enjoy work that they are invested in and that fulfills them and helps them develop and grow.
- People want to use their talents to benefit the organization and make a difference.

When projects succeed because of some of these beliefs, discuss how these beliefs lead to success. Again, actions tend to speak louder than words. People will tend to adopt different beliefs when they see leaders adopt them and when they see how they have led to results in situations that they also experience.

Here are some of the beliefs we've heard that might undermine trust:

- People are lazy. If not watched, they will not work diligently [Lal14].
- People work for money [Lal14].
- Demanding something will make it so [Ken Schwaber, in Del15].
- People are selfish and put their interests above those of the organization [Lal14].
- Teams want to run away from work [Ashish Pathak, in Del15].

- People need to be told what to do, when to do it, and how to do it. They also need to be held accountable [Lal14].

The differences are very similar to Douglas McGregor's Theory X and Theory Y.

3.5 Example: How to destroy a high-performing team

David on management culture clashes

One of the stories that I tell about trust centers on my first job as an instructional designer. I was the tenth hire in a small training startup called Horn Interactive. As the new hire, I was given the desk in the elevator hallway as a joke. New people were being hired monthly (so that I could quickly pass on my elevator seat as a rite of initiation) and after a little more than a year we grew to more than 50 people.

As a small team, we grew to know each other quite well. We all sat within shouting distance of each other and if someone wasn't going to work out, everyone knew it well before it happened. Many of us would do things together outside of work, and I'm still in contact with most of the group and friends with several.

Our startup had a couple of differentiators. First, we had people who knew the technical world. I was one of these people. I could explain complex technologies like multiprotocol routers or voice over IP (VoIP) to non-technical audiences. At the time, these technologies were quite new and people questioned whether VoIP could compete with traditional telephony.

Second, we hired extremely talented graphic designers from a renowned local graphic-design program. The e-learning that we developed looked more like video games or comic books or photorealistic simulations than much of the existing cookie-cutter, low-end graphic HTML. To do this high-end development required time and effort and teamwork between the instructional designers, customers, subject-matter experts, and our graphic-design team.

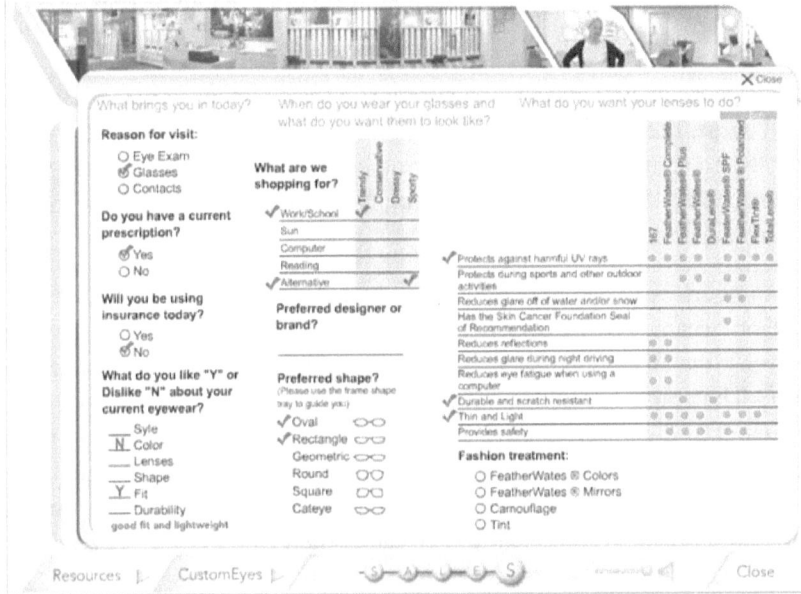

Figure 3.6: Screenshot from photorealistic sales simulation.

The graphic designers, most of whom were fresh out of college, quickly became their own high-performing team. They took over a room in the back of our office, became fast friends, shared much of the same culture, and focused on clients. One of the ways they bonded was through playing video games like Quake. They also had a private mailing list where they would joke around with each other and play Photoshop wars.

As our group grew, one of the people who rose to a management position was an instructional designer who had some unfortunate history with the graphic-design team. He didn't see the value in their play. Instead of seeing these activities as bonding, brainstorming, and letting off steam, he viewed them as "not working". Think about how much more work they could get done if they would simply stop playing Quake.

He decided the graphics team needed a manager who could instill discipline in the group so he hired a former Air Force captain. The graphic designers saw this as bringing in someone to police them. One of the first things the new manager did was institute a morning team status meeting to discuss tasks. The manager wanted to know what was going on and the status of individual projects. The graphic designers saw this meeting as a one-hour waste of time because they knew what was going on and all the meeting did was take away an hour that they could be spending on graphic design.

The manager insisted on being put on the designers' private mailing list. Of course, they immediately stopped using the list to discuss all things related to their close-knit group. Sometimes this involved issues with other people that they would sort out. Now, they were being scrutinized by management.

As someone who had to work with the graphic-design team, I found that my job became more difficult. Now, there were sides where before there weren't: management, instructional designers, graphic designers, and editors. The graphic designers wanted to know who you sided with — management or them. The answer was really both or neither. The lack of trust had suddenly become an organizational issue. Instead of a single team focusing on the customer, we started to become two teams that required rules and protocols for dealing with each other. And these rules and protocols had consequences in terms of speed and cost.

Some of this dysfunction was related to our growth as a company. Some of the dysfunction came from personal issues between the graphic-design team and the newly appointed manager.

To his credit, the Air Force captain recognized the dynamics of the situation. He didn't want to be a babysitter. He quickly positioned himself for another role in the company and recommended that a graphic designer lead the graphic-design team.

Others within our organization suggested forming more project-focused teams organized around specific customers and projects. These teams consisted of a project manager, instructional designers, graphic designers, and editors.

As these customer-focused teams formed and people again worked closely together on shared customer goals instead of in functional groups, trust grew and we re-established our business around highly performing small teams.

The lesson I learned from this experience was that sometimes self-organizing teams develop their own cultures and their own ways of doing things. Bringing in someone from outside to "manage" an already high-performing team can be perceived as violating trust.

PART
FOUR

Responsibility

"A hero is someone who understands the responsibility that comes with his freedom."

— Bob Dylan

4.1 Relationship to trust

One way to think of responsibility is the flip side of a coin that has trust on the other side. When we trust, we look for responsibility in return — and when people trust us, they look for responsibility.

The agile principles codify this relationship:

> Build projects around motivated individuals. Give them the environment and support they need, and trust them to get the job done.

Motivated individuals are responsible individuals. Trust them to get the job done.

A common, semi-humorous piece of advice for new managers consists of three rules:

1. Get good people.

2. Give them a goal.

3. Get coffee and donuts.

"Get coffee and donuts" means get people what they need to be successful. These simple principles are both serious and humorous because although they are easy to say, accomplishing the three often takes a great deal of work.

In *The Agile Culture*, Pollyanna Pixton, Paul Gibson, and Niel Nickolaisen have a great chart that illustrates the relationship between trust and responsibility or, as they call it, ownership [Pix14].

On the trust and responsibility chart, Energy & Innovation is the desired quadrant; this occurs when there is high trust and high ownership. The chart also illustrates, however, where things can go wrong and easily turn into Failure, Conflict, or Command & Control.

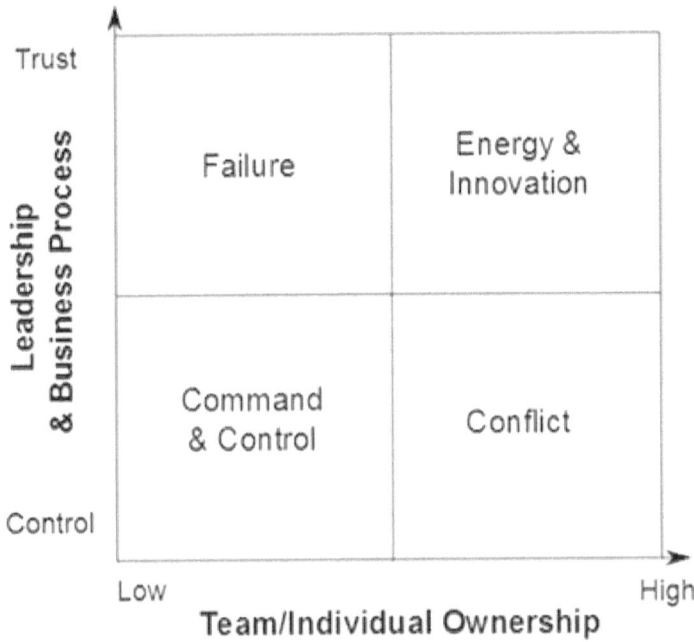

Figure 4.1: Trust and responsibility.

In this chart, trust is depicted as coming from leadership, and responsibility is envisioned as coming from teams and individuals. We like to think of it as a feedback loop between any two groups.

Thinking about trust and responsibility as a feedback loop is useful because it can help demonstrate why accomplishing the three simple manager rules can be so difficult.

If you've ever been to a concert or performance and heard the screech of an amplifier when a microphone is turned up too high, you've experienced what's known as positive feedback. In the world of electronics, positive feedback often is undesirable. What happens is that a sound that was fed into the microphone gets amplified and projected and the microphone records it again. This quickly escalates into the screeching sound you hear. In this instance, feedback boosts the signal until it overloads the amplifier.

Negative-feedback amplifiers, on the other hand, are amplifiers that subtract part of the output from the input. In this manner, part of the feedback opposes the original signal. What this process does is increase the system's stability. Because of this advantage, most amplifiers today are negative-feedback amplifiers. These amplifiers can still be overloaded, however, if a microphone or other input device is turned up too high or is placed too close to the output.

What does all of this mean in terms of trust and responsibility?

It means the two have to be in balance. And that balance can be difficult to achieve. This is why, of course, people often joke about how easy it is to manage projects. It sounds easy. In reality, the balance between trust and responsibility takes care and experience to achieve.

The relationship can fall out of balance when something goes wrong. There's temptation, especially from managers or former managers, to step in and institute more control to remedy the situation. To others, this feels like responsibility is being taken away, and trust decreases. With the decrease in trust comes a fear of making mistakes and decreased performance.

Another way the relationship can fall out of balance is if a team isn't sure who has responsibility for a certain task. A clear lack of responsibility can erode trust between team members when tasks aren't accomplished.

On the flip side, when the relationship is in balance, truly amazing things can happen.

David on the balance between trust and responsibility

A pharmaceutical client wanted to teach the managers of their sales teams certain techniques that had been proven to work in the field. They wanted to do this in a way that would let managers practice what it was like to do things both incorrectly and according to best practices.

We proposed building an online simulation that modeled what sales managers faced. Sales managers would have a simulated team of performers at different levels and during each sales cycle they would determine how to allocate resources. A sales cycle would then play out and they could make adjustments. Over time, they'd see how their strategy was doing. Sometimes top sales representatives would leave. Or a manager would have to decide what to do with low-performing account managers. The client loved the idea and wanted it to be very realistic.

What we didn't mention to the client was that we had never built something quite like this before. We had done similar simulations and thought it was possible because we had a high-performing team that trusted each other and shared responsibility.

Figure 4.2: Screenshot from pharmaceutical simulation.

The development team scoped the project as a stretch, but doable. The team believed they could do it and everyone had good working relationships with each other from past projects.

The trust and responsibility the team had built up allowed us to believe we could do things beyond what we had been done before.

As development progressed, the team's creativity started to show. The programmers and graphic artists created unique visual icons and images to represent resources and the sales team. The writers had fun scripting backgrounds and looking for people to do the voices of the characters. We designed an interface that would take players through calendar quarters and years.

The end result exceeded what any one person on the team could have designed, and the customer absolutely loved the finished simulation. It modeled real situations that sales managers faced, allowed them to try different strategies in a safe environment, and provided relevant feedback that helped them learn. It was much more powerful than simply relating recommended sales strategies. The simulation taught and reinforced best practices in a fun and believable way.

This is the type of result that a high degree of responsibility and a great deal of trust can produce.

4.2 Aspects of responsibility

Briefly, Table 4.1 shows are some high-level aspects and signs of responsibility in organizations and their importance to agile.

Aspects of Responsibility	Importance to Agile
Autonomy/ Freedom	Autonomy is, in part, freedom to make decisions and take appropriate action. It is also the environment and support needed to turn decisions into value for the customer.
Motivation	Motivation is typically an individual goal that aligns with the goal of the team to delight customers. It may include money but more likely than not, it has to do with what a person wants to be and enjoys doing.
Commitment	Commitment is necessary to deliver working increments frequently. It also allows teams to gauge velocity.
Mutual Responsibility	Mutual responsibility is responsibility to others. The focus on customer needs, excellence, timely delivery, and teamwork requires thinking beyond the individual. Agile self-organizing teams are teams of leaders.

Table 4.1: Aspects of responsibility.

The next four sections look more closely at these aspects.

4.2.1 Autonomy and freedom

Commander's intent is a military key concept in 21st-century military operations. It is a clear, concise statement of what the commander wants to achieve and why.

The United States Army Field Manual describes it:

> The commander's intent is a clear, concise statement of what the force must do and the conditions the force must establish with respect to the enemy, terrain, and civil considerations that represent the desired end state. The commander's intent succinctly describes what constitutes success for the operation.

The idea behind commander's intent is that leaders of various units know that constitutes success for a given mission. What is the desired result? This allows staff and subordinates to figure out how best to achieve this result.

Commander's intent was modeled after the German concept of *Auftragstaktik,* developed in response to Napoleon's method of waging war. Lieutenant Colonel Lawrence G. Shattuck describes the philosophy of *Auftragstaktik* [Sha00]:

> At its foundation was the realization that battle is marked by confusion and ambiguity. The German army leaders consciously traded assurance of control for assurance of self-induced action. These leaders developed a military cultural norm that supported and expected decisive action by subordinates in the face of uncertainty or ambiguity. Fundamental to the success of *Auftragstaktik* in the German doctrine was trust.

The military is probably not the first thing people think of when they think about autonomy or freedom. In many ways, this assumption is quite true. There is a very rigid command structure in the military and when recruits join the military, they agree to dress similarly, obey orders, and act within this structure.

However, when it comes to the battlefield, the U.S. Army found that its officers simply could not plan for every contingency. The future and the enemy are simply too unpredictable. The idea behind commander's intent is that, if the original plan fails, people still understand the mission. Soldiers are free to improvise to achieve the desired objective.

Colonel Tom Kolditz, the head of the Department of Behavioral Sciences and Leadership at the U.S. Military Academy, offers this example: [Hea07]:

> Suppose I'm commanding an artillery battalion and I say, "We're going to pass this infantry unit through our lines forwards." That means something different to different groups. The mechanics know that they'll need lots of repair support along the roads because if a tank breaks down on a bridge the whole operation will come to a screeching halt. The artillery knows they'll need to fire smoke or have engineers generate smoke in the breech area where the infantry unit moves forwards, so it won't get shot up as it passes through. As a commander, I could spend a lot of time enumerating every specific task, but as soon as people know what the intent is they begin generating their own solutions.

Agile similarly emphasizes this level of simplicity: "the art of maximizing the amount of work not done is essential." Autonomy and freedom to get the job done are essential in commander's intent. By definition, commander's intent specifies the "what" and allows individuals to figure out the "how."

In addition, freedom, in an agile sense, is not simply the ability to make decisions. All the good decisions in the world won't make a difference if people don't have support. Freedom, from an agile view, is also the environment and support needed to get the job done.

Here are some questions to ask about autonomy and freedom in an organization:

- At what level are people free to make decisions? What types of decisions?
- When goals are established, are teams free to determine how to get there?
- How are goals communicated within the organization? Who is responsible?
- Are teams responsible for how goals are achieved?

4.2.2 Motivation

The agile principles discuss building projects around motivated individuals. The initial collecting of motivated people can be handled through good hiring practices. The way organizations motivate people after they've been hired is part of organizational culture.

Motivators can be categorized as intrinsic or extrinsic. Intrinsic motivators are internal and related to what individuals enjoy while extrinsic motivators are rewards or incentives. Another way to think of extrinsic motivators is carrot-and-stick motivators: punishment or reward.

Figure 4.3: Examples of intrinsic and extrinsic motivators.

Oddly enough, intrinsic motivation as a concept is relatively new, first documented in the 1950s in an experiment involving monkeys. Harry Harlow, a professor of psychology at the University of Wisconsin-Madison, noticed that monkeys began playing with puzzles he placed inside their cage without any rewards or teaching. The puzzles were simply placed inside the monkey cages and pretty soon, through trial and error, the monkeys solved them. The two main motivational drives known at the time, biological and extrinsic drives, failed to explain the monkeys' behavior.

Harlow theorized that the monkeys enjoyed the task and called this "intrinsic motivation" [Har50].

Edward Deci, a graduate psychology student at Carnegie-Mellon University in the late 1960s, found similar results years later in a puzzle experiment with humans [Dec85]. Deci also compared intrinsic motivation with monetary reward and found that monetary rewards could hinder intrinsic motivations if they were offered and then taken away:

> Subjects who had been paid for working with an intrinsically interesting activity were less intrinsically motivated following their

experience with the money than were subjects who had done the same activity without pay.

Later experiments found that participants who had received money rated the puzzles significantly less enjoyable.

Both Deci's and Harlow's results ran counter to the theories of the day that people were "coin operated", and these findings still encounter resistance in certain realms, such as economics where extrinsic motivation is an assumption of many economic models.

This isn't to say that extrinsic motivation isn't a factor. Rather, it isn't the *only* factor. Especially when it comes to tasks that involve creativity or innovation.

Daniel Pink, in his book *Drive: The Surprising Truth About What Motivates Us*, writes about three types of intrinsic motivators for complex projects: autonomy, mastery, and purpose [Pin09a]. We've already covered autonomy as an aspect of trust and mastery/craftsmanship as an aspect of responsibility.

In terms of purpose, what motivates people to take responsibility to do extraordinary things?

It helps to discuss a pattern best explained by Simon Sinek with his Golden Circle diagram. Sinek's presentation *How Great Leaders Inspire Action* is the number one viewed TED Talk as of 2015 [Sin09].

Sinek explains that every organization knows what they do: they offer a product or sell a service. Some organizations know how they do it. These organizations typically add some kind of value to their product or service that sets them apart from the competition. Very few organizations, however, know why they do what they do.

"Why" is typically a purpose, cause, or belief.

Sinek argues that great organizations think from the inside out while average organizations think from the outside in. The example he uses is Apple.

If Apple were like most organizations, their marketing message might sound like this:

> We make great computers (what). They're beautifully designed, simple to use, and user friendly (how). Want to buy one?

We say what we do and we expect some kind of inspired action. This approach is typical for most of us.

Figure 4.4: Sinek's Golden Circle.

Instead, Sinek says, Apple communicates like this:

> We believe in challenging the status quo and thinking differently (why). The way we challenge the status quo is by making our products beautifully designed, simple to use, and user friendly (how). We just happen to make great computers (what). Want to buy one?

In Apple's case, people buy what Apple stands for: innovation.

Sinek argues that the goal is not to do business with everybody who needs what you produce. The goal is to do business with people who believe what you believe.

If you don't know why you do what you do, and people respond to why you do what you do, how will you ever get people to want to be a part of what it is you're doing?

This question is why starting from beliefs is so important and critical. This is why agile starts with a manifesto. This is why agile begins with "why".

Agile believes in "uncovering better ways of developing software by doing it and helping others do it."

Similarly, if your organization understands why they are doing what they're doing, why they're building what they're building — whatever that is — people will tend to take more responsibility and ownership, especially if they believe in the goal, belief, or cause.

Typically, people in an organization understand what they are doing and how they are doing it. Some questions to ask about motivation within an organization are:

- Do teams and individuals understand why they do what they do?
- Do individuals understand why their group does what it does and how this relates to the overall mission of the organization?
- What societal ideas about a better world are similar to or different from the organization's mission?

David on Instinctive Drives

There are a number of different self-assessments that teams can use to help understand individual intrinsic motivations. Cisco used the Instinctive Drives profile [Bur07].

Our group found this profile particularly helpful because it focuses on what motivates people instead of on their personalities. If you want to get along with someone, it helps to understand their personality. However, when you need to figure out how to work with someone, understanding what motivates them is more useful.

The Instinctive Drives profile has four categories: Verify, Authenticate, Complete, and Improvise. An assessment provides rates each of these four areas from one to nine to produce a four-digit number that indicates what motivates you. It also provides information about what you tend to value most when working on a project. High and low numbers in these categories don't correspond to good or bad but rather to different motivations.

For example, people who have high Improvise scores like new challenges, pressure, and dynamic interaction. They commit easily to projects without needing time to think through them. People with low Improvise scores thrive on certainty, logic, and time to think.

Instinctive Drives is not a personality test or behavior analysis, but rather a window into someone's intrinsic drives.

For example, a person who is a high Verify without a counterbalancing lower score in another category is a person who has a strong drive to get things right. This person desires perfection and to work out the correct way to do things at the correct time in order to be correct. She will enjoy analysis, evaluation, and coming up with strategies and will want time to consider all of the options. She will function best when she is in control and she might have a critical streak that makes her focus on the few steps that could have gone better instead of the pieces of the project that went well. Analysis paralysis might also be an issue.

While not a high Verify person myself, I have worked with many instructional designers, trainers, programmers, project managers, and graphic artists who fit this profile and who thrived on details and analysis. High Verify was actually the most common profile on our development team.

Understanding that high verifiers thrive on analysis helped me to hand off analysis portions of projects. I find that arguing with high verifiers is difficult and often unproductive. They can appear dogmatic when what is really going on is that, in their minds, they've worked out the solution to the problem and have settled on an answer. High verifiers like to have feedback, but they can be stubborn if they believe they've figured out the solution. In situations when I've had a different view, I learned to first always provide positive feedback on what I liked and then ask questions where I thought we could do better. This approach allowed high verifiers to build their case or to see their work from a different angle and allowed me to avoid head-to-head arguments. Sometimes I convinced them, sometimes they convinced me. Either way, we avoided a fight and focused on what would make the project better. While asking questions is important with everyone, it's especially important with people motivated by the need to verify because they pride themselves on being correct.

Similarly, when I shared my own profile with team members, I would tell them that I was a "high Authenticate". This means I'm very hands-on and I need to visualize things and believe in them before committing fully. I'm also driven by honesty and trust in relationships. I like interesting projects and I like to learn new things. Sharing this type of information about our intrinsic motivations with team members often helped us figure out who might want to do what on a particular project.

I talk about Instinctive Drives as a skeptic of personality profiles. I've completed Myers-Briggs and a couple of other personality profiles and never found this information about people to be very useful. By comparison, I found an understanding of what motivates people far more valuable, especially when it could be freely shared.

This fits in with a comparative study that looked at Myers-Briggs and Instinctive Drives. The research, conducted by Geoffrey Chapman at the University of Western Sydney, concluded that the difference is likely related to what the two assessments are trying to measure [Cha08]:

> The instructions of the MBTI [Myers-Briggs Type Indicator] are likely restricting the results to only observed behavior, whereas the instructions of the ID System questionnaire, combined with ranking system used in the questions allow some degree of motivation to be measured. In short, a possible difference between these two measures could be that the MBTI is limited to measuring what people do, and the ID System is attempting to measure why people do what they do.

4.2.3 Commitment

For change to firmly take hold in any organization, there has to be commitment. Chris Argyris, a professor at Harvard Business School, spent much of his life looking into why organizations struggle to change despite the knowledge that they need to change [Arg98]:

> To understand why there has been no transformation, we need to begin with commitment. Commitment is not simply a human relations concept. It is an idea that is fundamental to our thinking about economics, strategy, financial governance, information technology, and operations. Commitment is about generating human energy and activating the human mind.

Argyris makes a distinction between external and internal commitment. One way to think of this difference is how it pertains to someone who starts his own business and someone who goes to work for another company.

Who is more motivated and by what? Almost certainly, the small business owner is going to be more motivated because she is defining every aspect of the business. In this situation, employees often don't feel responsible for the way the situation is defined because it has been defined for them.

Internal commitment, by comparison, comes from within. Internal commitment is what religious leaders like Rick Warren talk about when they say "a sense of purpose". When people internally commit, they commit based on their own motivations. They commit because they are good at a particular task or they want to try something new or they simply love what they're doing.

Argyris uses Table 4.2 to further outline the differences:

External Commitment	Internal Commitment
Tasks are defined by others.	Individuals define tasks.
The behavior required to perform tasks is defined by others.	Individuals define the behavior required to perform tasks.
Performance goals are defined by management.	Management and individuals jointly define performance goals that are challenging for the individual.
The importance of the goal is defined by others.	Individuals define the importance of the goal.

Table 4.2: External and internal commitment.

While Argyris argues that it's unrealistic for everyone to allow thousands of people to fully participate in self-governance, agile takes the belief in commitment a step further and states that "The best architectures, requirements, and designs emerge from self-organizing teams."

While many interpret this statement as specific to software, it is agnostic in terms of what is being developed so long as what that is has changing requirements or is dealing with something new that hasn't been tried before.

Self-organizing teams are teams within which commitments must be made. When I speak about agile to people outside of the agile community, one of the first questions is how do people know what to do.

The answer is commitment.

Self-organizing teams define their own tasks, individuals take ownership for how tasks are to be accomplished, and the teams prioritize how work is going to be accomplished. Thomas and Meghan Cagley, in "Much Ado About Commitment", write "The act of committing to the work, saying what you are going to do and then doing what you said, provides both transparency and a feedback mechanism."

As Argyris discusses, the act of defining tasks and then committing as individuals to the team for certain tasks creates a huge sense of empowerment. Within the team, there is a sense of freedom that allows people to take on tasks that they want to work on for reasons of their own choosing.

Not only does commitment help people understand who is responsible for what, it also helps the team adjust if, for whatever reason, priorities change or there is under or overcommitment. Traditional project-management methodologies would place the emphasis on the project plan. Instead, agile acknowledges that the plan is ever changing.

What types of commitments do teams and individuals make? How? Do people on the team know who is responsible for what?

In an agile implementation, such as Scrum, the team makes a series of commitments. In Scrum, the goal of these commitments is to deliver the highest prioritized value to the customer as quickly as possible. As the team progresses, commitments are adjusted. In this manner, teams can also quickly welcome inevitable changes in requirements.

Many project managers new to agile and implementations like Scrum struggle with the agile idea of ongoing, short, dynamic development. The concept of commitment can help them with what they perceive as loss of control. One role of project managers in an agile environment could be to help the team keep track of commitments. Instead of committing to a project plan, teams figure out their own commitments (who is responsible for what) in short, iterative time periods with the goal of quickly delivering value.

For this reason, Scrum includes commitment in the Scrum code of ethics: "We take responsibility for and fulfill the commitments that we undertake — we do what we say we will do."

In agile, the idea of commitment goes beyond simple agreements within the team. It allows teams to unlock the energy of entrepreneurship and empowerment. It gives people the freedom to pursue what they want to pursue within the context of self-organizing teams.

4.2.4 Mutual responsibility

Up to this point, we've discussed the individual aspects of responsibility. In an agile culture that focuses on collaboration between business people and on self-organizing teams, responsibility for others is also a key organizational value.

The movie *We Were Soldiers*, based on the real-life experiences of Joe Galloway and Lieutenant Colonel Hal Moore, features one of the best examples of mutual responsibility on film [Sim11]. In a training exercise, two officers deal with a similar situation in two completely different ways.

Figure 4.5: Mel Gibson as Lieutenant Colonel Hal Moore in We Were Soldiers.

The first officer notices that one of his men, Godboldt, is favoring his left foot. At a stopping point, he asks the soldier and all of the other men to take their boots off. Examining the soldier's foot, he realizes it's raw and blistered from chafing. He tells Godboldt to draw some fresh socks from supply and keep his feet dusted with powder to keep them dry.

He also tells the other soldiers to pair up and to similarly check each other's feet. After identifying the solution, he made the team responsible for fixing it. He didn't say he was going to solve it for them. He showed them how to solve it and enlisted their help in taking responsibility for the team.

Moore observes another officer leading his team up a hill. This officer also notices one of his men is falling behind. By contrast, this officer shouts at the soldier, "Why were you in the back? Goddamn it, why were you in the back?"

Both officers faced the situation of a soldier falling behind. The first leader saw his role as identifying the cause of the problem and working to fix it. He asked questions to figure out that the issue was chaffing from wet shoes. After he identified the problem, he suggested a solution. He also communicated the solution to the rest of the team. He didn't blame anyone and he accepted responsibility for helping out the entire team.

By comparison, the second officer blamed someone on his team for being weak without trying to understand if there was an issue. In the first situation, the officer made sure to focus on the problem and not the person. This is a key aspect of mutual responsibility: accept the person even when the person is struggling. Show and teach people how to improve in areas where you can help and when you learn new things. In return, ask for help in areas where you see others are strong. This is how teams grow and become better.

Some questions to ask about mutual responsibility in organizations are:

- Do people accept responsibility for their actions?
- Do people respond defensively or feel threatened?
- When issues are encountered, how does the team react? Do they work together to solve challenges? Or do they place blame?
- Do people feel responsible for others on the team?

4.3 Common organizational beliefs about responsibility

As discussed previously, beliefs — things that people find "true" — often influence values. When creating an organizational culture that emphasizes responsibility, work to reinforce beliefs that lead to responsibility and challenge beliefs that may undermine responsibility.

Here are some beliefs that you want to emphasize and work towards in organizations to drive home the importance of responsibility:

- People are responsible for their decisions and actions.
- People are reliable, self-motivated adults capable of making important decisions.
- Everyone has what they need to succeed [Pix14].

- Everyone is a leader with responsibility.
- Mistakes are accepted, not punished [Pix14].
- Responsibility for making decisions should be with those closest to the information [Sin14].
- Accept people even when performance may need improvement [Bret Simmons in Del15].
- We are responsible for others as well as for ourselves.
- People have a good sense of what they can and can't commit to.

By contrast, here are some beliefs that might undermine responsibility as an organizational value:

- Managers are responsible for decisions.
- Leaders hold positions of power.
- People are lazy. If not watched, they will not work diligently [Lal14].
- People work for money [Lal14].
- People are selfish and put their interests above those of the organization [Lal14].
- Teams want to run away from work [Ashish Pathak in Del15].
- People need to be told what to do, when to do it, and how to do it. They also need to be held accountable.
- Without leadership, teams act like mobs [Sur04].

If people see someone's performance is lagging, this can cause issues on a team. People can feel resentful that someone isn't contributing as much he or she should be. This is one reason why implementations of agile, such as Scrum, emphasize the role and importance of a coach.

Coaches can step in and help identify impediments and issues, and can work with the team to find resolutions. Rather than directing individuals, coaches look to understand issues and people and work with them and the team to remove impediments and come up with solutions. This, when taken seriously, is often a full-time role.

PART
FIVE

Learning

"Experience is simply the name we give our mistakes."

— Oscar Wilde

5.1 The world is unpredictable

Is the world too complex for people to predict global events?

Philip Tetlock asked this question in his 2005 book *Expert Political Judgment* [Tet06]. Tetlock looked at expert opinions from 1984 to 2003 and quantified how well their forecasts turned out compared to amateurs. Some 300 experts submitted more than 28,000 specific, quantifiable predictions about the future. Tetlock came to some startling conclusions. First, experts performed better than random chance but only marginally better. And second, what mattered more was not what they thought, but how they thought.

The first issue, however, is not the experts. It is the complexity of the world we live in.

Paul Ormerod, a British economist, compared the extinction model of dinosaurs to that of businesses [Har11]. He found that, although the time-lines were different, extinction patterns were similar. He also found that when he modeled corporations as successful planners, he wasn't able to duplicate what happened to businesses in real life. Patterns of extinction were completely different in models that viewed corporations as successful planners. What his models imply is that there is little correlation between the amount of planning a firm does and success.

What both Tetlock's and Ormerod's results suggest is that in these situations where the future is largely unknown, trial and error and the ability to learn from experience is essential. In many areas, however, learning from experience and adapting is often viewed as a weakness.

In politics, for example, people often admire certainty and intractability over adaptability. Senator John Kerry was characterized as a "flip flopper" for supporting the wars in Iraq and Afghanistan after speaking out against the war in Vietnam upon his return from active duty in 1971. President George W. Bush, who on the other hand vowed to "stay the course", was re-elected. In 2006, Jean Schmidt, a freshman congresswoman from Ohio, claimed "cowards cut and run." Prime Minister Margaret Thatcher similarly declared, "You turn if you want to. This lady's not for turning."

In courtrooms in the United States, we see the CSI effect: juries that have unrealistic expectations about what forensic evidence can and cannot do. By 2012, the *CSI* television show was seen by 67 million Americans a week. Oregon lawyer Josh Marquis described the CSI effect this way [Car15]:

> Jurors now expect us to have a DNA test for just about every case. They expect us to have the most advanced technology possible, and they expect it to look like it does on television.

Trial lawyers often adapt their techniques to take into account this CSI-effect-driven desire for certainty [Dys12].

In mathematics, the math that we learn first is the certain math. We start with math that helps us balance our checkbooks and figure out how to get to our jobs on time. We learn how to calculate. We learn how to compute. It's not until much later in most curricula that proofs and more abstract mathematics are taught. Many people do not even know of the types of problems that can't be solved easily or have no known solution within mathematics.

The P vs. NP problem — listed as one of the seven millennium problems by the Clay Mathematics Institute (CMI) — is such a problem [For09]. CMI describes the problem this way:

> Suppose that you are organizing housing accommodations for a group of 400 university students. Space is limited and only 100 of the students will receive places in the dormitory. To complicate matters, the dean has provided you with a list of pairs of incompatible students, and requested that no pair from this list appear in your final choice.

It's easy to check if a solution satisfies these criteria. However, the task of generating all of the possible solutions seems just about impossible because the number of ways of choosing 100 students is greater than the number of known atoms in the universe. It's believed that this is beyond the reach of even the most powerful supercomputers of the future. However, no one has yet proved these problems to be unsolvable in a reasonable amount (polynomial amount) of time.

Similarly, predicting the future is an example of a problem that is, in all likelihood, beyond the capability of any supercomputer now or ever. There are so many variables and the system is so complex that a computer would need to recreate the world to predict the future.

If the future is unpredictable, why do we spend so much time planning? Why do we value certainty so highly?

Part of this desire for certainty comes from running a business. If we know how much something costs, we know how much to charge and therefore we can run a business at a profit. With complex projects, however, as we've seen, our best guess is likely that, a best guess.

Agilists believe that trying to plan any but the most simple of projects from beginning to end is impossible.

This belief is sometimes misunderstood as not believing in planning. Agilists do believe in planning, they simply believe it's better to spend your time planning in small increments than it is to try to plan an entire complex project before it starts.

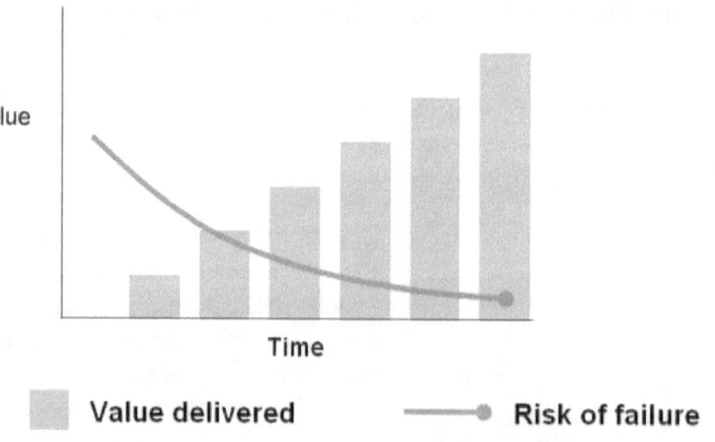

Figure 5.1: Delivering value in small increments reduces risk.

One way to visualize this is in the value graph in Figure 5.1, which shows how delivering value in smaller increments leads to gradual reduction in risk. A traditional project has a higher risk of the project failing at the end of the project.

By approaching complex projects in small increments, it is easier to see early on what adjustments need to be made. What is valued is the ability to adjust and to adapt when predictions inevitably fail.

Agile speaks to Tetlock's conclusion that the world is often simply too complex for accurate prediction. When it comes to complex projects, we know there are likely to be many failures along the way. The important thing is that we learn to revise and adapt as we progress.

It's easy to make this statement. Everyone is familiar with phrases like "success always starts with failure" but there are often conflicting motivations within organizations that value predictability and forecasting. Finance departments want to know budget forecasts, CEOs need quarterly revenue forecasts, and managers often want exact deadlines.

If learning and improving are not viewed as a way of doing business, organizations will not develop the ability to adapt.

5.2 Aspects of learning

Briefly, Table 5.1 illustrates some high-level aspects and signs of learning organizations and their importance to agile.

Aspects of Learning	Importance to Agile
Risk	If the highest priority is to satisfy the customer, teams have to have the ability to try different paths without fear of reprisal.
Feedback	Feedback allows teams to continuously improve. At regular intervals, teams reflect on commitments, risks, and results, and use this to learn and become more effective.
Adaptability	Once a team takes a risk and receives feedback, how does the team adapt? Adaptability is important to meet changing requirements.
Sharing	In order to adapt quickly and respond to ever changing customer needs, lessons learned need to spread throughout the organization.

Table 5.1: Aspects of learning.

The next few sections look more closely at these aspects.

5.2.1 Risk

Learning involves a certain amount of risk and tolerance for mistakes.

While it's important to manage risk, people also have to have a certain amount of freedom to try new ideas and new things with the knowledge that many of these things will fail. The way agile manages risk is to take small steps and adapt along the way.

Thomas Edison is perhaps the classic example of the value of experimentation. Edison created the first research lab or "skunkworks" in Menlo Park, N.J. in 1876.

Figure 5.2: Upstairs at Menlo Park.

Known primarily for inventing the phonograph, the first practical electric light bulb, the kinetograph and kinetoscope (early motion picture technologies), and a system for distributing electricity using direct current, Edison held more than 1,000 patents.

Some of his lesser-known inventions included cement houses complete with cement furniture and cement pianos, the electric pen, and vacuum packing.

Edison's process was one of intense trial and error.

In the January 1921 issue of *American Magazine*, Edison described a conversation he had with a dispirited associate [For21]:

I recall that after we had conducted thousands of experiments on a certain project without solving the problem, one of my associates, after we had conducted the crowning experiment and it had proved a failure, expressed discouragement and disgust over our having failed to find out anything. I cheerily assured him that we had learned something. For we had learned for a certainty that the thing couldn't be done that way, and that we would have to try some other way.

To Edison, mistakes were just part of the learning process. Because of the unknown nature of his explorations, he held a high tolerance for making mistakes and risk.

More recently, Cisco Systems pioneered a strategy for taking risks called the "spin-in". A spin-in is a separate company financed solely through a single investor, in this case, Cisco.

In 2012, Cisco invested $100 million in a spin-in called Insieme with the option to buy it for $750 million. Insieme created Cisco's next-generation product, the Nexus 9000, to move Cisco into the market-disrupting world of software-defined networking (SDN). SDN has the potential to disrupt Cisco's $21-billion routing and switching business.

Figure 5.3: Cisco Nexus 9000 Series [Cis 14].

Insieme went from startup to sale in 21 months.

The idea was pioneered with one of Cisco's early acquisitions. A company called Crescendo Communications had pioneered a network switch that threatened to displace Cisco routers. In 1993, Cisco purchased Crescendo Communications, and the network switch evolved into Cisco's Catalyst

6000 and 6500 series switches. Cat6 switches became one of the most successful networking products ever.

Cisco's CEO John Chambers commented on the acquisition in 2014 [Ser14]:

> In 1993, we made our first acquisition... and the stock went down. I paid about $92 million on a company with a couple million in revenue. It generates $13 billion in revenue today with great gross margins.

With the Crescendo acquisition, engineers Mario Mazzola, Prem Jain, and Luca Cafiero joined Cisco.

In 2001, these three engineers were funded to start the first spin-in (Andiamo Systems) to enter the storage-networking market. Andiamo developed Cisco's first Fibre Channel storage-area-network (SAN) switch — the MDS 9000 series. In 2006, the team was tapped again to create Nuova Systems. Nuova created the data-center servers that would become Cisco's Unified Computing System (UCS).

In each case, Cisco recognized a need to move outside Cisco operations to develop a new product. With respect to SDN, *Business Insider* wrote [Mcl13] that "Cisco's corporate culture has too many fiefdoms, too much politics, to build such an important product in-house."

Cisco needed a fast-moving startup that would allow engineers to take big risks and move quickly within a safe environment.

The Nexus 9000 that Insieme developed was also a new technology that replaced hardware functionality with layers of software. At the time, Cisco didn't have enough software experts. Insieme could more easily hire specialized software expertise.

Both Edison's skunkworks and Cisco's spin-in strategy are examples of agile environments for developing complicated or complex products.

Agile, as a philosophy, is designed for projects whose customer requirements are changing or whose technology is new. In these types of situations, a certain amount of trial and error needs to take place. Valuing risk allows teams the freedom to experiment.

To help evaluate tolerance for risk within an organization, ask:

- Are people encouraged to seek out new ideas and try new things?

- How does the organization define innovation? How do leaders view mistakes and risk?
- What happens when people make mistakes? Are they shut down when something doesn't work? Is it safe within the culture to take risks?
- How does the organization provide new opportunities and challenges?

5.2.2 Feedback

PlayPumps were merry-go-rounds designed with the idea kids at play could put their energy to good use pumping water from a well.

The PlayPump would pump water from a well and into a storage tank while kids were playing on it. This water could then be easily dispensed at other times. When PlayPumps were introduced in Africa in 2005, they generated a tremendous amount of excitement because it seemed like an ingenious way to harness something kids were already doing for good.

Figure 5.4: Picture from a PlayPump advertisement.

PlayPumps were advertised as huge improvements over the hand pumps Africans struggled with for years. First Lady Laura Bush announced that the U.S. government would donate $16.4 million for installation of Play-Pumps across southern Africa [Cos10]. Steve Case, the founder of America Online, pledged $5 million. Jay-Z filmed a short piece that aired on MTV to try to raise even more funds. PlayPumps became a popular cause.

Pictures abound online of happy kids playing on PlayPumps. On the surface, it seems like a great idea. The problem is that no one really asked anyone on the ground about how these were working.

Owen Scott is a Canadian engineer who blogged about his experiences in Malawi. Blogging online about the PlayPumps in 2009 [Sco09], he asked:

> How often do you get to hear about the results of a development project from the people who are actually using it? Not that often. Most of what you hear gets filtered through layers of PR. Well, with this post, I'm trying to change that. It might end up being a bit anticlimactic, but read on for an on-the-ground consumer review of a new piece of "development" technology.

Scott drove to see one of the PlayPumps in action and arrived to find two women struggling to turn the merry-go-round. The water was being pulled up into the tank (which wasn't full) before it came down into their buckets.

When the PlayPump had been installed, the hand pump that used to exist was removed in the name of progress.

Owen asked one of the women if she preferred the hand pump or the PlayPump. The woman responded that she far preferred the old hand pumps because they were easier to use and filled buckets quicker.

Scott compared how long it took each to fill a 20-liter bucket:

> Traditional hand pump: 28 seconds

> PlayPump: 187 seconds

The purpose of this discussion is not to denigrate the inventors of the PlayPump. On the contrary, we need people to take chances with new ideas. The purpose, rather, is to highlight the importance of receiving good feedback at the appropriate time.

In this case, the right feedback came from villagers using the PlayPumps as they would every day (not when Western journalists were taking pictures) and comparing the performance to that of traditional hand pumps.

When thinking about feedback within organizations, ask:

- What mechanisms exist to provide feedback?
- How do people know when something isn't working?

- What types of feedback are acted on and how?
- How easy is it in the organization to ask questions and receive honest answers?

Feedback allows teams to continuously improve. At regular intervals, Agile teams reflect on the commitments they made and the risks taken and the results and use this to learn and grow.

Michael on the Dunning-Kruger effect

One of the fascinating things about agile is that things can appear to get much worse before they get better.

This often happens because of the dual burden of the Dunning-Kruger effect. In brief, the Dunning-Kruger effect states that people with poor skills in an area do not only reach erroneous conclusions and make unfortunate choices, but their incompetence robs them of the ability to recognize that they are doing that.

In other words, the skills that lead to competence are often the very same skills needed to evaluate competence. People who do something poorly may also vastly overestimate their skill in an area.

David Dunning and Justin Kruger, psychology researchers at Cornell, also found that those who were competent at a skill were better at assessing their own performance [Kru99].

One of the experiments was in the domain of humor. Humor requires sophisticated knowledge about culture and tastes. In this study, they presented people with a series of jokes and asked them to rate the humor of each one, and then they compared these self-ratings to the ratings of professional comedians.

Dunning and Kruger found that people estimated their ability to be 66% on average, 16% above the 50% mean value awarded by the pros. Interestingly, as performance improved, the ability to predict one's own performance also improved. Most egregiously, those whose performance was worst tended to overestimate their own skills by 46%.

At the top level of performance, people actually underestimated their own ability. Experts often have greater knowledge of what they still don't know and tend to be more humble about their own abilities.

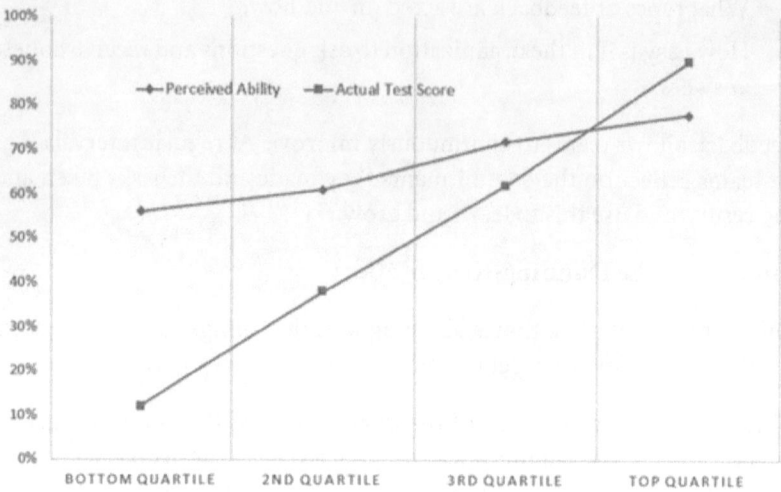

Figure 5.5: Perceived ability to recognize humor compared with actual ability as determined by professional comics [Kru 99].

This tendency is true about learning as well. The same skills that allow you to learn or not learn are the skills that allow you to self-assess correctly.

The people who don't learn don't have the skills to self-assess and so they have an inflated sense of their own ability. Experts at learning have the ability to self-assess and are more likely to feel that they always have more to learn.

In a company new to agile, the Dunning-Kruger effect may be reflected in early retrospectives. That is, an organization that is not agile and starts to become agile may see poor initial retrospective scores as the team's perceptions of excellence change.

In an organization that is authentic and has an understanding of excellence, what happens is that the scores might initially get worse. The team is actually improving — but because their understanding of excellence has jumped by an order of magnitude, the team members are judging themselves against a much higher standard.

For example, many teams will say that they're doing a great job of collaborating. What they often mean by this is "we're nice to each other." When they start learning how true collaboration works, how it's different from cooperation, and how they should be realizing results much greater than any individual alone could achieve, their collaboration scores drop.

A person who views collaboration as "being nice to each other and not arguing" might rank the team high so long as they're nice to each other and not arguing. However, those on the team who are actually trying to collaborate and detect problems are probably scoring the team much lower because they have started to see their potential. They're scoring the team based on a new definition of excellence that can lead to greatness whereas the former person is stuck in niceness.

Organizations new to agile who see an immediate improvement typically have very low standards and are simply doing a better job of meeting these low standards. In many cases, as observed with Dunning-Kruger, these teams simply don't have the metacognitive ability to recognize that they are poor performers.

This is why it's so important to have coaches that are able to accurately assess where teams are at and who are familiar with high-performing teams. Also crucial is a culture that allows these coaches to openly and honestly provide feedback both to the team and to management.

In any agile transformation, it's important to set this expectation with executives. Inform them upfront about the Dunning-Kruger effect and that scores might initially get worse as people come to comprehend what excellence means.

The consultants and agile coaches that you want to look for are the coaches who will have the courage and authenticity to say these types of things rather than someone who tells you "we will get you the metric you want to get" within 30 days or some other period of time. As soon as someone guarantees success, it means no learning is going to take place.

5.2.3 Adaptability

Prioritizing adaptability as a value is clearly stated in the Agile Manifesto where "responding to change" is prioritized over "following a plan." This allows for the second agile principle:

> Welcome changing requirements, even late in development. Agile processes harness change for the customer's competitive advantage.

Examples abound of companies that missed opportunities because they failed to meet customers' changing needs. A few prominent examples include:

- Kodak
- Xerox
- Digital Equipment Corporation
- Atari
- Wang
- Motorola
- Lucent
- Blockbuster
- Borders

Many of these companies had developed technology ahead of customer trends. Kodak, for example, developed the first digital camera in 1975, light-years ahead of any other company. The company was even quicker to market. The Digital Camera System (DCS) and consumer-brand DC series appeared in the early 1990s. However, Kodak's bread-and-butter business was still print film and the company thought digital cameras would cannibalize its own business.

Figure 5.6: A Kodak DC220 digital camera with zoom [Tig09].

Kodak was correct to think that digital cameras would change the film business forever. Unfortunately, as a company, they fought this trend rather than embrace it. By the time they released their EasyShare point-and-shoot cameras in 2001, they were behind the market instead of ahead of it.

Xerox failed to capitalize on many of the successes their Palo Alto Research Center (PARC) developed, including the personal computer, the mouse and graphical user interface (GUI), laser printing, an Ethernet LAN, and a WYSIWYG (what you see is what you get) text editor.

Douglas Smith and Robert Alexander in their book *Fumbling the Future* highlight some of the reasons why Xerox failed to commercialize the PARC lab inventions [Smi88]:

- Xerox perceived itself as a copier company.
- No effective methods existed to transfer technology from PARC to the manufacturing and sales groups at Xerox.
- There was a culture clash between Xerox management and the inventors at PARC.

These are some examples of what Harvard Business School professor Clayton Christensen calls "the innovator's dilemma" [Chr97].

Christensen distinguishes between two types of technological advancements: sustaining technologies and disruptive technologies. Sustaining technologies are the innovations we are traditionally familiar with, innovations that make products better, innovations that improve the performance of existing products. Disruptive technologies, on the other hand, are innovations that tend to result in worse performance, at least initially.

Disruptive technologies have a different value proposition: we'll give you something similar for a good deal less. As Christensen writes: "Products based on disruptive technologies are typically cheaper, simpler, smaller, and, frequently, more convenient to use."

Digital cameras are an example of a disruptive technology. Smart phones are an example of a disruptive technology. Streaming video is an example of a disruptive technology.

Disruptive technologies don't simply fit into an existing market. Disruptive technologies create new markets that threaten and often overwhelm traditional markets if organizations fail to adapt.

On the flip side, companies that have adapted include:

- Apple
- IBM
- PayPal
- Google

- Intel
- DuPont
- Berkshire Hathaway
- Disney
- Johnson & Johnson
- Toyota

IBM is a classic example of a company that remade itself around its services business as it experienced first the death of its mainframe computer business and then the falling margins associated with its personal computer business.

Charles O'Reilly, director of the leading change program at Stanford's Graduate School of Business, calls it "organizational ambidexterity": the ability to manage current business while simultaneously preparing for changing conditions [Kra13]. A more common term for this is "adaptability", and adaptability is valued within companies like Toyota and Johnson & Johnson.

Some questions to ask about adaptability in organizations are:

- Are disruptive technologies recognized?
- How difficult is it to take a different direction? (This could be targeting a different market, looking at new technology that might hurt your current business, or examining the ways you do business in light of new trends and disruptions.)
- At what rate is your organization improving? (If the rate is not greater than your competitors, all it does is delay your demise.)
- What happens when someone suggests a different approach in response to changing conditions or requirements?

In the situations discussed, companies had developed new technologies in advance of the market. The difference between success and failure was whether the organization valued adapting at a point in time when it didn't seem like the organization needed to adapt.

Agile accepts that customer requirements change. New requirements are critical to a customer's business and, as we've seen, even survival.

5.2.4 Sharing

Speed and solving customer issues are perhaps the two biggest keys to technical support. Every incoming call is going to be a customer with an issue.

To help technical-support staff, companies usually keep a knowledge base of common and uncommon resolutions to customer issues. New associates are taught that 80% of questions tend to correspond to 20% of issues. They are also trained how to search the knowledge base when a customer raises an unfamiliar issue. The knowledge base, in addition to standard troubleshooting procedures, is usually the first option for front-line technical-support staff.

Tier 2 and higher support staff tend to be more experienced associates with advanced troubleshooting skills and technical expertise in certain product areas. They often contribute articles to the knowledge base when new issues are resolved. Many companies, such as Apple, put much of their knowledge base online so that customers can instantly search for help to common problems.

Figure 5.7: Screenshot from Apple Support website.

Within the technical-support group, knowledge is often shared quite well because all members tend to be co-located with easy access to higher-level tiers of support. Sometimes, this communication breaks down between the technical support and engineering. High-tech companies truly interested in delighting their customers tend to have ways for technical support and engineering to communicate with each other; either engineers are involved in the technical-support organization or tech-support quickly relays new problems they can't solve to engineering.

Consider an organization that operates charter schools. What if they could help teachers share best-practice materials so each teacher didn't have to create their own materials each time?

Kim Oakes, director of sharing and communities of practice for the Knowledge Is Power Program described organizational learning this way [Mil11]:

> We know that about 80% of our teachers create materials from scratch. It became increasingly important to connect our teachers, so that they could build upon one another's ideas rather than work in isolation.

If an organization doesn't have mechanisms in place to capture, share, and distribute best practices and lessons learned, the organization is unlikely to improve. Organizations should have similar mechanisms in place for learning as individuals: experience, memory, and sharing.

Some questions to ask about sharing in organizations are:

- Where is knowledge created and located?
- How are best practices captured, shared, and adopted?
- How does the organization encourage individual development? Team development?
- What divides exist within the organization and how is communication established between these divides?
- Are teams and individuals rewarded for sharing?
- Are agile teams becoming inbred so that they can't share across teams or functions? How often do great ideas "hop ponds"?

Agile is predicated on the basis of small teams. Sharing within teams is built into the philosophy through daily communication and reflecting on how to become more effective. Sharing and mechanisms for sharing will help agile scale as an approach in larger organizations and will allow best practices and ideas from smaller teams to spread company-wide.

Michael on the Core Protocols

The Core Protocols are a set of commitments and protocols Jim and Michele McCarthy introduced in the book *Software for Your Head*. The protocols came from their experiences at Microsoft and their shared interest in creating great teams and great partnerships. The Core Protocols cover topics such as commitment, how to make decisions so that good ideas triumph over egos, and asking for help.

You can enter into a Core Protocols agreement with anyone: a team of software developers, your family, your friends, or whomever.

One of the protocols is asking for help. You can ask for help as many times as you want. Part of the rationale is that you want to ask for help before you actually need help. The person asked can say agree to help or decline, and you don't question his response. It's a clear and explicit protocol for asking for help.

In many environments, asking for help is viewed as a transaction that involves a form of mental accounting. You think you can ask for help from a person because you've helped her in the past. Or, you'll agree to help this person because you know her and she has helped you in the past.

Implementing specific rules helps to eliminate this accounting. You can ask for help as many times as you want and you can turn down requests without feeling bad about it. The simplest way to think about this is that asking for help is no longer viewed as a burden. It merely becomes something that you do within the group of people who have committed to the protocols.

What's interesting to me about this is that I'm a professional at this and yet I noticed a radical difference between formally entering into this agreement with someone and the relief and ease and support it gives me versus informal relationships with other people such as coworkers, friends, or other consultants.

I don't feel like there's an accounting system where I've asked someone for help 23 times and have only helped him 17 times in return.

In an informal situation, there's a tendency to wonder "Am I interrupting this person?" or "Will that person think I'm stupid?" if I ask for help. If I ask for help now, what is that person going to want? Will the person tell someone else about my question?

Many corporations and organizations have implicit rules about asking for help. Some people know them and some people don't. Those who know the rules are often able to accomplish things seemingly effortlessly, while the unaware struggle and often have their ignorance held against them. People won't help others who don't follow the implicit rules as much because they feel they are being asked in an incorrect manner, even though these rules are never written down.

With the Core Protocols, the rules are known.

We often say, "There are no stupid questions." However, we also know that this maxim tends not to be true. There are stupid questions. And people are judged by the questions they ask. Especially in group settings.

With the Core Protocols, the rules are known, which makes it unbelievably easy to ask for help and to provide feedback.

5.3 Common organizational beliefs about learning

As discussed previously, beliefs or ideas that people hold "true" often influence values.

Here are some of the beliefs to emphasize and to work towards in organizations to emphasize the importance of learning and improving:

- The future is complex and ever changing.
- Confusion is the start of learning something new. People are often confused just before a learning breakthrough.
- People care about learning and want to improve.
- Mistakes are the process of learning.
- If you're going to fail, fail as quickly as possible and learn from it.
- Learning is a continuous process.
- Learning can come from anywhere and anyone.
- Different people have different learning styles: visual, logical (mathematical), experiential, aural (auditory-musical), verbal (linguistic), social, or solitary.

By contrast, here are some beliefs that might undermine learning as an organizational value:

- The future is predictable.
- Confusion is bad [All14].
- People don't care about learning and people don't want to improve.

- Errors or mistakes are bad and should be punished.
- Projects shouldn't be started until everything is planned out.
- Failure is not an option.
- Training is required for learning.
- Instructors are the source of knowledge.
- Silence means understanding.

5.4 Example: Dedicated learning time

Michael on the amount of time experts spend learning

Years ago, I went to a Microsoft conference with lots of well-known speakers. I made it a point to ask each speaker what percentage of their time they spent formally learning. I'm not talking about on-the-job learning, I'm talking about formal learning. Reading a book, taking a class, or saying I'm going to learn about something new or improve my skills in an area I want to work on.

The average was 33%.

This figure is shocking compared to averages for corporate America. Of a year, 33% is roughly 17 weeks. Compare this to recent average published in the Association for Talent Development's *2014 State of the Industry* report [Mil14]:

> On average, large organizations report that their employees received 36 hours of training, approximately 4.5 days. Midsize organizations report that their employees received 27 hours of training, almost 3.5 days.

Those 4.5 days are less than 2% of the year. That's how much time the average large organization encourages its employees to spend on training.

Google famously advocated that employees spend 20% of their time on learning and side projects [Tat13]. Even though 20% time isn't a formal policy, it is part of Google culture and the fact that 20% of time spent exploring new ideas has led to Google News, autocomplete, Gmail, and AdSense.

One person I asked at the Microsoft conference, who was a leader in his field, told me:

> Michael, I'm afraid I'm going to disappoint you. I used to do a lot of learning, but I've now reached a senior position and I have a family. So I'm comfortable where I am professionally and I want to spend more time with my family. So I only spend about six hours a week learning.

Some people who are genetically gifted with high intelligence are able to translate this skill into learning on the job, but many people who become thought leaders are simply people who have been able to prioritize learning.

Companies like Google make learning a priority by making learning part of the culture, whether the rule is a formal rule or not.

There is enormous pressure in a work environment to do exactly what we did yesterday because we're always in emergency mode. The important thing is to build the widget in the way we know how because we have to have five widgets by tomorrow. If we spend any time learning how to build widgets better, we're going to miss that deadline.

Of course, this puts us on a treadmill, where we never learn. We're always in emergency mode and not learning. As a result, teams might not be delivering optimal results. More significantly, because teams are not learning, they're never going to improve and deliver better results.

What was fascinating to me was that the people who are writing the books, the authorities and thought leaders in the field, spend from 15% to 33% of their time learning.

For software developers, learning should be part of their job. The job shouldn't be to code. It should be to learn how to code better. If teams aren't learning, they're not doing their jobs. The culture should encourage learning with dedicated time and resources.

PART
SIX

Collaboration

"No one can whistle a symphony.
It takes an orchestra to play it."

— Halford E. Luccock, professor of Homiletics, Yale Divinity School

Several people, including Jean Tabaka and Michael Sahota, have written about the importance of collaboration to agile using William Schneider's cultural model from *The Reengineering Alternative*. Schneider's model considers four distinct cultures [Sch94]:

- Control: This is a typical hierarchical model in which people follow the chain of command. Control corresponds to red and amber organizations in Laloux's evolution of organizations.

- Competence: The competence model is an entrepreneurial or meritocratic model. In this model, decisions are typically made by a few experts. Laloux characterizes this model as orange.

- Cultivation: A cultivation culture is primarily driven by values. The focus is on growth and accomplishment with a sense of purpose. In Laloux's model, cultivation is green.

- Collaboration: A collaboration culture focuses on teamwork, connection, valued input, and consensus. A collaboration culture is similar to a teal or green culture in Laloux's model.

Schneider, similarly to Laloux, discusses the strengths, pitfalls, and types of work appropriate to each rather than claim one cultural type is better than another.

In 2010, Michael Spayd, managing director of Collective Edge Coaching, surveyed 120 people from the agile community and asked them about their culture [Spa10].

Collaboration was cited the strongest cultural preference (47%) for the ideal agile team, followed closely by cultivation at 41%. Competence and control were a distant third and fourth.

This finding is not surprising given agile's emphasis on self-organizing teams, individuals and interactions, and customer collaboration over contract negotiation.

At the very least, a cultivation culture doesn't interfere with agile adoption the way a control or competence culture likely would.

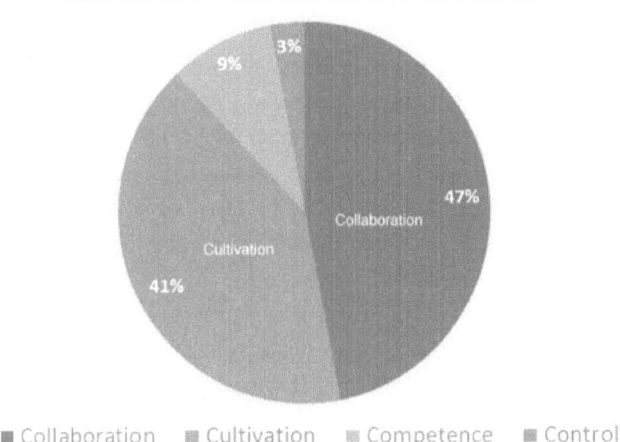

Figure 6.1: Michael Spayd's survey of agile cultures, May 2010.

Also, not surprisingly, many others have discussed the importance of collaboration to agile. Tabaka, in *Collaboration Explained: Facilitation Skills for Software Project Leaders*, argues for the importance of facilitated collaboration [Tab06]:

> I learned a few things: facilitation has a place in how we create teams and coax collaborative work from and for them. Additionally, I learned that facilitation is not about control or manipulation. Rather, it is about applying tools, techniques, and processes in support of teams eager to engage in high performance. Good facilitators listen and echo in a way that helps a team hear itself and apply its best wisdom. Project managers and software team leads with facilitative skills become leaders who can listen and echo as they lead teams in vision and success.

An organization that not only values collaboration but understands how to successfully collaborate is critical to agile.

6.1 Collaboration compared to cooperation

Organizations often misinterpret collaboration as either cooperation or design by committee.

A quick example should help illustrate the difference between collaboration and cooperation.

A large software company was launching a new product after an acquisition. It became clear that the product-development team at the acquired company had not worked closely enough with sales and marketing to be able to support the launch. Sales and marketing knew there was going to be a launch, but because they hadn't been involved in the planning sessions, they struggled to come up with the appropriate marketing and training to support the launch. As a result, the launch went through on time, but didn't really gel for about six months. The company lost many sales opportunities during those six months because the sales force wasn't willing to chance selling something it wasn't prepared for and didn't see as proven.

In this situation, the different teams had only played nice with each other and kept each other informed but were not working together to help each other succeed at the overall goal of delivering a proven product that could hit the ground running with customers. It had all the appearances of collaboration, but the groups weren't really working with each other. This became apparent as the launch date approached and sales and marketing failed to produce the key pieces that should have materialized. For example, sales had requested from pilot customers case studies that demonstrated benefits and returns. Sales viewed the case studies as must-haves. The development team didn't see them as a priority and assumed sales could get them quickly after launch with little impact.

The product development team had kept marketing and sales informed but hadn't engaged them in a joint effort. This led to a great deal of scrambling when it was discovered that expectations for launch were very different on each side.

What was lacking in this effort was synchronization of resources and goals. Had these groups gotten together early in the process to figure out what they wanted to build, who was going to commit to what, and what took highest priority, the groups would have truly been collaborating. As it happened, the groups were merely cooperating.

In collaboration, all of the collaborators should be involved to discuss the overall goal, approach, and commitments. As Ron Ashkenas wrote in *Harvard Business Review* [Ash15]:

> One of the biggest mistakes that managers make is trying to foster what we might call "serial collaboration", i.e. going from one func-

tion to the next and trying to cobble together an agreement. Not only is this time consuming, but it rarely works since each change affects the next.

Similarly, collaboration has gotten a bad reputation because in the past it has meant design by committee. In *The Wisdom of Crowds*, James Surowiecki wrote [Sur04]:

> This "can't we all get along" approach exacerbated the problems created by the seemingly endless layers of management that most corporations acquired in the years after World War II. Paradoxically, in trying to make the decision-making process as inclusive as possible, companies actually made top executives more — not less — insulated from the opinions of everyone else. Before any decision could be made, it had to make its way through each layer of the management hierarchy. And since at each level the decision was vetted by a committee, the further you got from the front line, the more watered down the solution became. At GM, for instance, something as relatively straightforward as the design of a new headlight had to be considered in 15 different meetings, and bizarrely, the CEO of the company sat in on the last five of those.

In an agile environment, collaboration means something quite different from cooperation or this idea of inclusion (where everyone's opinion must be considered) [Sur04]:

> Collaboration needs cooperation. True collaboration, however, is where the product of the whole is greater than the sum of the parts.

In *Coaching Agile Teams*, Lyssa Adkins describes collaboration this way [Adk10]:

> The ideas that emerge don't come with a straight-path way to trace back to their origin. When collaborating, team members build on top of one another's ideas, each person giving away their cherished vision of what it "should be" so that something better, something that no one of them could have imagined alone, emerges from the ash of their burned and forgotten personal visions. This creates an environment of courageous sharing and vulnerability, an environment where the whole truly can be greater than the sum of its parts.

This emergent property is the end goal of agile collaboration.

6.2 The agile framework for collaboration

If we look at the first four agile principles, we can see the framework for setting up collaboration:

1. Our highest priority is to satisfy the customer through early and continuous delivery of valuable software.

2. Welcome changing requirements, even late in development. Agile processes harness change for the customer's competitive advantage.

3. Deliver working software frequently, from a couple of weeks to a couple of months, with a preference to the shorter timescale.

4. Business people and developers must work together daily throughout the project.

The agile development team commits to the highest level of customer satisfaction and to address changing requirements, even late in the development stage. To meet these commitments, business people and developers must be involved daily throughout the project. The level of involvement is not specified, but there must be close involvement and feedback to ensure stages of development deliver the most value.

The Agile Manifesto also values "customer collaboration over contract negotiation" because contract negotiation, as British economist Ronald Coase wrote, contains transaction costs that include costs of bargaining and decision, policing and enforcement, and search and information [Coa60]. When you can work together with a customer and both sides trust that each is working in the other's best interests, you can reduce this overhead and reach decisions faster.

In terms of how internal teams collaborate, agile considers face-to-face conversation as the most efficient and effective method of conveying information. This requirement leads to smaller teams, typically of fewer than 10 members. If a project demands more resources, an agile approach would be to break the project into smaller components that could be worked on in small teams and introduce coordination between the smaller teams.

6.3 Aspects of collaboration

Table 6.1 briefly shows some high-level aspects and signs of collaboration in organizations and their importance to agile.

Collaboration	Importance to agile
Transparency	Transparency allows vision into decisions for all team members and leads to people trusting each other and collaborating.
Self-organization	The best architectures, requirements, and designs emerge from self-organizing teams.
Communication	The most efficient and effective method of conveying information to and within a development team is face-to-face conversation.
Unity/Alignment	Collaboration involves working together towards a shared purpose or goal. Cooperation is working on separate goals and then trying to cobble results together.

Table 6.1: Aspects of collaboration.

Subsequent sections look more closely at these aspects.

6.3.1 Transparency

In the story "The Emperor's New Clothes", Hans Christian Andersen described inauthentic behavior that's common to many organizations. In the story, two crooked weavers convince an arrogant emperor that they have a fabric that the ruler can use to judge people for new positions. The suit they make for him will appear invisible to anyone who is either unfit or too stupid for the position.

The Emperor loves the idea — he can use his new suit to figure out who is competent and who is not! Wary that the weavers might be cheating him, he sends his top advisor to look at their work.

Of course, the advisor doesn't see any work on the loom and wonders if he's too stupid to see it. Not wanting to appear incompetent, he says, "Oh, it is magnificent!"

Late into the night the crooks pretend to weave on an empty loom. Other advisors sent to observe also praise the magnificent cloth. Soon, the entire city is talking about it.

Figure 6.2: Weavers pretending to weave with invisible cloth [Han89].

When the emperor parades before his subject in his new clothes, everyone compliments the wonderful fit and the beautiful colors — until a child says, "But he doesn't have anything on!"

The rumor spreads that the emperor is wearing no clothes, and even the emperor hears it. Too proud to admit the truth, the emperor keeps marching, with his followers carrying the hem of the clothes that aren't there.

In the development world, this scenario happens all the time. Chris Argyris, expert in organizational behavior, characterized this as inauthentic behavior and said it is quite common, even among change experts [Arg90]. The causes are many and various and include corporate culture, compensation systems that punish honesty, and the human tendency to simply avoid conflict and unpleasantness.

A classic example of inauthentic behavior is project-status meetings where red, yellow, or green indicators are used to rate specific project tasks. The idea sounds good in theory: assign responsibility for tasks to the team and then ask individuals whether the task is tracking.

The reality tends to be much different, however. On a team call, everyone reports that their tasks are green — even if there are problems. Why? Because project sponsors want the project to be under control and reporting yellow or red is often interpreted as "out of control". In reality, all projects are yellow until they are completed. Therefore, green has little meaning except to pacify sponsors who want everything to be under control.

Everyone recognizes this dynamic and no one wants to sound like their portion of the project is not in their control in front of everyone else. So people typically report green status even when things are not green.

This means that project managers who use this method probably don't have nearly the level of transparency that they believe they have, not because anyone is particularly dishonest but simply because of how they are asking for information.

Compare this approach to a Scrum implementation of agile. In a Scrum implementation, teams meet daily for 15 minutes. Each team member answers three questions:

- What did you do yesterday?
- What will you do today?
- Are there any impediments?

Rather than providing a status to a project manager, the meeting is designed to allow the team to understand what work has been created and what remains. No boss is collecting information about a schedule. It is understood that aspects of the project are always yellow until they are complete.

By understanding that impediments are a normal part of the process and asking about them in a meeting designed solely for the team, the ScrumMaster (coach) can identify issues as quickly as possible and work to resolve them, either personally or by finding the appropriate person to resolve the issue.

Ray Dalio, founder of Bridgewater Associates, holds what he calls "radical transparency" as one of his core values. In an interview with *Leaders Magazine*(vol 33, no. 3, 2010), he described why this is important:

> My most important principle is that getting at the truth, whatever it may be, is essential for getting better. We get at truth through radical transparency and putting aside our ego barriers in order

to explore our mistakes and personal weaknesses so that we can improve.

Some questions to ask about transparency in an organization are:

- How does the organization address impediments within teams? Across teams?
- Is there a common etiquette within the organization and does this etiquette allow for transparent communication?
- At what level are development teams involved in business decisions? Or internal business organizations with development?

6.3.2 Self-organization

Perhaps the most interesting aspect of the Agile Manifesto is the principle that "the best architectures, requirements, and designs emerge from self-organizing teams."

In 2006, nurses in the Netherlands led what could be called a grassroots revolution against a nationwide neighborhood home-health-care system that emphasized paperwork and micromanagement over time spent with patients [Mon13].

Before this revolution, nurses were allocated a specific amount of time for each procedure, from administering a shot to bandaging an arm. The new rules treated the nurses like machines, focusing on maximizing the number of procedures performed and minimizing the amount of time for each procedure with the idea that this would deliver better health care.

One of the nurses described the system this way:

> The whole day, the electronic registration system that you have to carry with you is making you crazy. Some days I had to go and see 19 different patients. Then there is nothing you can do but run inside, put on a bandage or give a shot, and run out. You can never finish your work in a qualitative way. And when you go home, you keep thinking all the time, "I hope the nurse that comes after me doesn't forget to do this or that."

Not only were the patients lost in the administrative shuffle but so were the nurses.

In 2006, Jos de Blok, a former nurse in the system who was frustrated at the inability to effect change from within, created the model for the first team of nurses at what was to become Buurtzorg Nederland. Today, more than 8,000 nurses in four countries work for Buurtzorg in teams of up to 12 nurses.

Teams deal with all the usual tasks: establishing priorities, scheduling, planning, and making decisions. They do this as a team, however, with no boss. This could be a recipe for mob rule, dysfunction, or competition. Instead, Buurtzorg teams use specific methods to come to decisions. Before new nurses join a team, they take a training course called Solution-Driven Methods of Interaction, which teaches how solutions are adopted in meetings not based on consensus but rather whether anyone has a principled objection. If no objection exists, then the solution can move forward with the idea that a better one can always be brought forward later if new information surfaces.

In addition, each Buurtzorg team has a regional coach. Similar to Scrum-Masters, Buurtzorg coaches help teams self-manage. Their primary role is to remove impediments. They also tend to be experts at interpersonal skills and at asking questions to help teams come to their own decisions.

Each team develops its own personality and its own way of doing things. There are only a few ground rules that experience has shown is necessary for self-management. Some of these include:

- small teams of no more than 12 people per team;
- regular team meetings for communication and coordination; and
- periodic coaching meetings to discuss issues and learn from each other.

Karen Monsen and Jos de Blok write:

> If you give nurses autonomy, they'll organize their work in an effective way. Management is needed only to keep (1) the outside world outside, particularly if it's disturbing the work of the nurses, and (2) the collective ambition and organizational principles alive.

In an agile environment, collaboration is both individual and team-based. Collaboration is neither individual cooperation nor decision by committee. It is both working as a team towards a shared goal and an opportunity for individuals to do what they enjoy doing best within the context of the collaboration.

The idea is not to make everyone on a team equal. Of course, this will never be the case. Different people will bring different talents and skills to the table. The idea is to allow people to figure out and pursue and deliver what interests them most within the context of a team and organizational goals.

Figure 6.3: Jos de Blok, founder of Buurtzorg Nederland.

Questions pertinent to self-organization include:

- How do people organize and work implicitly? Are they handing work off or are they doing work together?
- Are talents understood within groups, and do people seek out experts?
- Do teams have access to resources as needed?
- What level of decision making are teams responsible for?
- What is the perception of what a team is and how it functions? Is teamwork perceived as being nice to one another?

6.3.3 Communication

What does communication mean in an agile culture?

Edward Tufte, professor emeritus of political science, statistics, and computer science at Yale, tells a great story about Louis Gerstner Jr.'s first days as CEO of IBM [Tuf09]:

> Gerstner had stepped into a meeting with Nick Donofrio, the executive in charge of IBM's mainframe System/390 business. Nick

had started running through his transparencies—the precursor to PowerPoint slides. When he got to slide 2, Gerstner stepped up to the table, turned off the projector, and said, "Let's just talk about your business."

The importance of this, as Tufte describes, is that talking is "an exchange of information, an interplay between speaker and audience."

By contrast, transparency slides and their modern PowerPoint equivalent are transmissions. They orient around the presenter instead of the content or the audience. PowerPoint is designed for one person to present his viewpoint to an audience.

Figure 6.4: A 2005 PowerPoint presentation by BP's chief scientist, Steven Koonin [Tai05].

Agile emphasizes a different type of communication, communication that is content-centric and audience-centric. The agile principles state: "The most efficient and effective method of conveying information to and within a development team is face-to-face conversation." Agile values conversation over presentation.

The other component of communication that agile emphasizes is continuous communication, both within the development team and between development teams and customers. Goals change quickly and communication is critical to deliver frequent value.

Comparatively, in traditional models, communication happens at certain stages of development. For example, in a kickoff meeting, teams might start with goals and objectives and developing a plan. Later, at certain points, the team might check in with a project manager or others on this plan. In an agile environment, team members collaborate closely to deliver value in increments, and active and continuous communication is required to adapt quickly to changes.

Questions to ask about communication include:

- How does knowledge circulate within the organization? Within teams? Between teams?
- How do people within and outside the group communicate?
- When someone needs something, how soon do they ask?
- How is feedback provided (on projects, on and to managers, to employees)?
- Can people joke with each other? Are people laughing and having fun? (Humor typically relies on shared values. When you hear people joking with each other, it's a sign that they know and trust each other.)

Michael on co-locating teams and handoff time

One simple thing that companies have discovered is that the handoff time between team members can dominate a project. The amount of time it takes to do the work can be small in comparison to the amount of time that no work is being done because work is being transferred from one person to another.

Person A hands off to Person B hands off to Person C. The handoff time can dominate the total time if teams are working from different locations, the nature of the user story requires many different developers or specialists, or there's a lack of clarity into what needs to happen.

In a simple example, let's say a programmer finishes a piece of a user story and sends it to a database developer in an e-mail with the note "I'm done." The database developer is doing something else and takes two or three days to get to the database component. While the developer might only work on the piece for, total calendar time elapsed is two days and an hour.

In scenarios like this, handoff time can easily consume 80% of total time and can dominate the overall project.

A particular company I was working for had decided to offshore its quality assurance (QA) to India. As a result, the software development team would drop the latest build on the development server and alert QA. The time difference would let QA flag defects overnight. If, the next day, the development team couldn't find one of the defects on their machine, they would e-mail QA to ask questions. Twelve hours pass. This back and forth takes a couple of days.

What the company found was that offshoring QA saved them on their cost per hour but it dramatically increased the number of handoff hours.

The company also had significantly invested in project managers to coordinate all of these handoffs. The project managers had an interest in keeping the offshoring arrangement because otherwise they'd have no purpose.

To the firm's credit, it realized that it would be better off co-locating QA. It took courage to reverse the previous decision but the VP of engineering made the change based on the data and co-located QA based on the feedback from the development teams.

To improve the speed of development, co-locating the QA team to reduce handoff time was simply a better, more agile option.

6.3.4 Unity and shared purpose

In 2008, hedge-fund manager Eddie Lampert purchased Sears. After purchasing the company, Lampert introduced a management model in which dozens of autonomous divisions competed with each other for resources.

Since Lampert's takeover, sales have dropped by more than $10 billion a year, Sears stock has sunk 64%, and its cash level is at a 10-year low.

Lampert argued that if the company's leaders were told to act selfishly, they would run their divisions in a rational manner that would boost performance.

Instead, as *Bloomberg* reported [Kim13]:

> The divisions turned against each other — and Sears and Kmart, the overarching brands, suffered. Interviews with more than 40 former executives, many of whom sat at the highest levels of the company, paint a picture of a business that's ravaged by infighting as its divisions battle over fewer resources.

Shaunak Dave, a former executive who left in 2012, says the model created a "warring tribes" culture where "If you were in a different business unit, we were in two competing companies."

As of the end of 2014, Sears had experienced 11 straight quarters of losses and was selling off assets such as Lands' End to try to generate cash. Lampert still seems unwilling to change course because of his fundamental belief that internal competition is best for the company.

In 1954, social psychologist Muzafer Sherif ran an experiment that could not be repeated today. He and his researchers recruited 22 boys for a three-week summer camp at Robbers Cave State Park in Oklahoma [She56]. None of the boys were told they were going to be a part of an experiment.

The boys were broken up into two groups called the Rattlers and the Eagles. During the first week of camp, in their separate groups, they did what most kids do at summer camp. They hiked, swam, canoed, and cooked out. By the end of the first week, each group had become a cohesive team.

The experiment began in the second week as the researchers introduced competition between the two groups. They played baseball games against each other and fought in tug-of-wars. Taunting began, first with name-calling and then with identifiers, such as a flag the Rattlers placed on the baseball field after winning a game. The Eagles burned the flag and put it back up on the pole. Fights broke out between the kids and they even raided each other's camps. After a week, the two groups viewed each other as complete enemies.

In the third week, the researchers wanted to see if they could reunite the two groups of warring kids. How did they do it? They introduced a series of seven unifying tasks that could only be achieved if the kids worked together.

First, they disabled a water tank and asked the boys to search the entire line in a coordinated effort to find the blockage. All the boys volunteered and eventually found the purposeful break and all helped remove the blockage. The researchers also forced a truck that was going to get food to need a push to start. They tied a rope around the truck and all the boys pitched in to give it a pull-start. By the end of this third week, the two groups of kids told stories and sang together around a campfire.

As in Sherif's experiment, when Eddie Lampert created competition among different Sears divisions, the divisions took on lives of their own.

The company doesn't seem to know what it's working towards other than competing for shared resources and attention.

Figure 6.5: Rattlers with banner reading "The Last of the Eagles" [She61].

The lesson, as Morten Hansen writes in *Collaboration* [Han09], is that leaders "have the power to unite separate groups by the actions they take. Leadership is, after all, ultimately about uniting people."

Similarly, career analyst Daniel Pink cites shared purpose — the yearning to do what we do in the service of something larger than ourselves — as one of the top-three motivators for businesses of the 21st century along with autonomy (self-organization) and mastery (craftsmanship) [Pin09].

Broadly, agile advocates for uniting around delivering value while leaving it to teams and organizations to determine what this means for different projects. The important takeaway is that unity and shared purpose are critical to collaboration.

A couple of questions that you can ask about shared purpose are:

- What processes are in place that create internal competition and do they have unintended consequences?
- If you asked 10 people from different groups, would each tell you a similar story about the organization's goals?

6.4 Common organizational beliefs about collaboration

As discussed previously, beliefs or things that people find "true" often influence values.

Here are some of the beliefs we've heard that you want to emphasize and work towards in organizations to emphasize the importance of collaboration:

- The best solutions emerge from self-organizing teams.
- Teams can accomplish more together than they can alone.
- Self-organizing teams are a different way of organizing (not a lack of organization).
- No man is an island.
- Teams unite around common goals.
- Collaboration is different from and preferable to cooperation.
- Communication is audience-centric and many-to-many (instead of broadcasts).
- Face-to-face conversation is the best method of communication for planning and decision making. Other methods might be preferable and faster for simple questions or communications.
- Excellence is more important than victory.

By contrast, here are some beliefs that might undermine collaboration as an organizational value:

- Individuals come up with the best solutions [Lal14].
- We don't need outside help.
- Internal groups/divisions should compete for resources.
- Knowledge is power (and consequently should be hoarded).
- Communication is a transfer of information (often from one to many).
- Victory is more important than excellence.
- Demanding something will make it so [Ken Schwaber in Del15].
- Teams want to run away from work [Ashish Pathak in Del15].
- Managers know more and are better at making judgments than their workers [Nigel Baker in Del15].
- Short-term advantage and gain is what matters.

- People do not want to be responsible for decisions [Lal14].
- People are selfish and put their interests above those of the organization [Lal14].

6.5 Example: Collaboration at Pixar

Ed Catmull, cofounder of Pixar Animation Studios, talks about how collaboration evolved and was recognized as the driving force behind their best films.

One of the amazing realizations that he talks about is how the first version of all Pixar movies sucks. In an interview with Diane Rehm on NPR, Catmull talked about his lessons [Reh14]:

> Well, here's the thing that we learned. And that is the first versions of all of our films suck. And it's — and I don't mean this in a self-deprecating way or that I'm being modest. What I mean is that they all suck. All right? They don't work.

This pattern held true for the original *Toy Story* movie, but Catmull and team didn't recognize the pattern until *Toy Story 2*.

The problem was that they had a script with a predictable ending. It was obvious Woody, the main character, was going to end up with his owner.

What Catmull realized was that his team was starting to fall into the pattern of traditional movie studios. Someone has an idea and a script and they make the movie based on the script.

> So we were starting to fall into the same pattern. We had a development group looking for ideas to be made into films. And we realized that with this one, the team wasn't functioning well together. Now, they were all good people. They all liked each other. But they were not a team where you could say that the whole was greater than the sum of the parts. When we put the original team on it, suddenly the magic happened. And it was at that point I realized, well, we've got this backwards.

His realization was that the key to great movies was not looking for ideas to turn into films. The key was building teams that were going to be able to solve problems because there were almost always going to be issues with the script. The key is building a team that makes the collaboration greater than the sum of the parts rather than a team that gets along well with each other.

Catmull provides another example from his experience with Walt Disney. He was working on a movie called *Bolt* whose main character was extremely difficult to animate. To finish the film, the Pixar team needed to redo the entire animation control system and Disney people estimated that would take six months to complete.

Figure 6.6: John Lasseter (left) and Ed Catmull (right) at the 2010 Visual Effects Society awards.

The film's release was scheduled for eight months in the future. Catmull got the team together and explained the principle of fixing things without asking for permission. Two guys spent a weekend remodeling and fixing the character and they had it back in production within a week.

What was the difference between one week and six months? Catmull said:

> The reason they predicted six months was they were building in mechanisms to prevent errors and failures. And all those mechanisms to prevent failure actually screwed things up. When all they had to do was make it, find the problems, find the little failures, and fix them. But that desire to avoid problems was so great that it was overriding common sense. Now, that's an extreme example, but it happens a lot.

It's the different mindset that can lead to greatness quickly. Or lead to failure quickly.

Either way, the team finds out if progress is being made or if a different direction is needed.

Pixar is going to take risks in the face of potential failure. Pixar created a safe, collaborative environment and culture so teams can focus on a goal and solving problems rather than getting caught up in planning or politics. Pixar teams collaborate towards greatness instead of simply cooperating or designing movies by committee.

PART
SEVEN

Agile Values
Revisited

"Culture is the process by which a person becomes all that they were created capable of being."

— Thomas Carlyle, Scottish essayist

7.1 Culture > process

Organizations are like icebergs: what we see above water is much less than what lies below.

Behavior, structures, and processes are what we see above the water. Below the water are the organization's values and beliefs.

We write about agile values in organizations to demonstrate the hidden aspects of culture that agile beliefs and principles should lead towards to achieve agility.

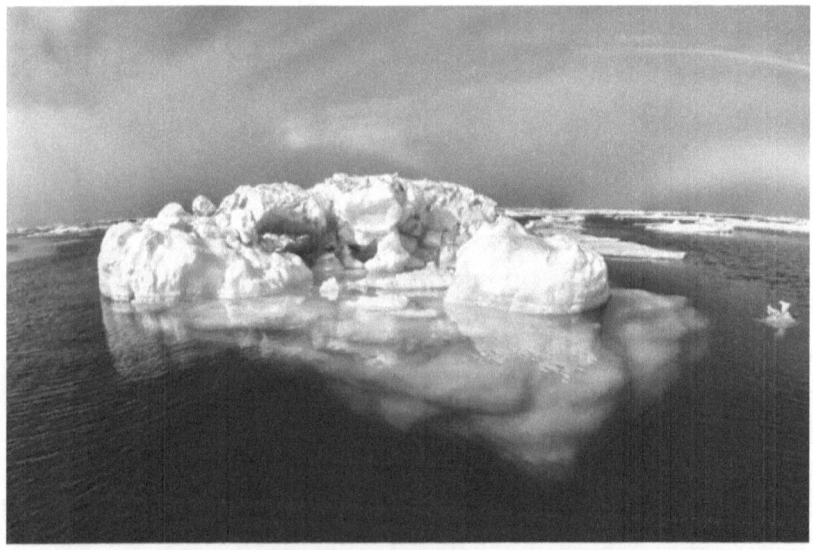

Figure 7.1: Iceberg encountered by NOAA Ship Fairweather in 2012 [NOA12].

Henrik Kniberg tells a great story about the evolution of Spotify. As a startup, the company started using Scrum and continued using it even as they grew to thousands of employees.

At a certain point, however, Spotify realized that the Scrum practices, the practices that they'd been following since inception, were actually holding them back [Kni13]:

> What we noticed was that we were following this process framework [Scrum] pretty much by the book, which worked quite well up to certain limits. After a while we grew to 15 or 20 teams. Now we have about 50 teams, but back then in 2010, it was maybe 15 teams. Always doing Scrum by the book, we felt, it was slowing us down. So we actually decided to screw the rules. This is actually a quote from one of the HR managers. He said, "Rules are a good start, then break them when needed."

What Spotify realized was that Scrum processes helped them create the culture. Once they had created that culture and recognized its importance, they could start to move beyond even Scrum processes.

Lyssa Adkins uses the Japanese martial-arts concept of *shuhari* to describe Spotify's experience [Adk10]:

- Shu*: Follow the rule.
- Ha*: Break the rule.
- Ri*: Be the rule.

This analogy is similar to Mike Cottmeyer's distinction between adoption and transformation, or the doing side of the equation and the being side of the equation. After you reach transformation or being, you have an agile culture.

Spotify achieved an agile culture and values. After reaching this stage, the company was able to break processes like Scrum to find new and even better processes for their teams.

Culture (beliefs, values, and principles), the much larger component of the iceberg, is what makes organizations truly agile.

7.2 If culture > process, why does change focus on process?

The simple answer is that process change is much easier. Changing a culture, especially a culture that's ingrained, is much harder. Culture can also be hidden and unacknowledged, or people within the organization might not know how to change culture.

The beauty of agile is that, as a framework for change, it provides a path for cultural change.

Instead of starting with processes, agile starts with a belief framework. Adopting these beliefs is the beginning of cultural change. Belief change leads to changes in values and subsequently principles. Culture changes.

The processes of Scrum (or other tools such as kanban) are simply ways to help surface some of the cultural dysfunction. Tobias Mayer writes in *The People's Scrum* [May13]:

> Scrum makes one promise only: It will help you fail in 30 days or less. That's it. Organizational dysfunction will begin to surface as the work plays out. Healing from that dysfunction is up to you. What Scrum can give you is a space to be human, to try, to fail, to reflect and to try again. Putting the Scrum framework in place at your organization will be the first step towards fostering an environment of safety and trust.

Mayer explicitly calls out how Scrum should lead to a culture change, a change towards an environment of safety and trust.

Processes and tools have been developed as starting points and ways to start being agile. These processes, along with coaching, practice, and support, can help teams transform to an agile culture.

However, if change ends at processes and the organization fails to recognize, for whatever reason, that the larger goal is culture change, transformation will fail. The real value of agile is this shift to agile values (if your culture is not already agile).

7.3 The agile culture and a few recommendations

The Agile Manifesto pulled beliefs above the water and made them visible. We took this a step further to show how agile beliefs lead to agile values and a more human-centered organization.

Rather than to present a comprehensive, all-inclusive view, our goal was to come up with a useful view of the agile "being" side of the equation. In other words, are there values or aspects that we didn't discuss? Sure. Do we think we covered the most important ones in a way that is simple and useful? We hope so.

Stephen Denning wrote "How to make the whole organization agile" for *Forbes* in July 2015 [Den15]:

> Resolving the tensions between agile and traditional management cannot usually be achieved by purely rational means. In part, that's because the traditional role of management often enjoys deep emotional attachments, attitudes, values, and views about how the world works, which collectively add up to a corporate culture or an ideology.

The shift to an agile organization isn't like purchasing a new productivity program and teaching it to new employees. It's also not like repairing an engine, when once the engine's fixed, it stays fixed. It's more like a heart transplant, where the organization's existing immune system — its culture — may work to reject the transplant. For this reason, it's important to understand the existing culture and the value changes agile leads towards.

Here are some final thoughts and recommendations for executives:

1. If you see agile as a series of processes that the IT team follows, you're missing the potential.

2. If there are change initiatives within your organization, agile, as a framework for change, can help.

3. If you are new to agile, bring in experienced leaders and/or coaches who can help guide you through the transition.

4. Self-organizing teams need help to self-organize (especially if agile is new). The coach role cannot be overemphasized because agile is a culture change, not a process change.

5. Agile might change your culture (and this is a good thing!). If you don't want a culture change, agile might not be right for your organization.

6. After an organization becomes agile, change should be significantly simpler with less overhead than required for periodic change initiatives.

7. Resources and budgeting for agile change should be similar to resources and budgeting for a major change initiative.

8. Executive support for agile should be similar to executive support for a major change initiative.

And here are some for coaches:

1. Executives might see agile as a process or tool. Help demonstrate the full potential and illustrate how agile is a framework for change.

2. Partial agile may be no agile. If adoption of agile is limited to the team level, it risks being incomplete and may not lead to the desired improvement.

3. Look to understand the elements of agile culture in your organization and where there might be opportunities to improve.

4. In any new transformation, if the culture is agile (teal/green in Laloux's model or Collaboration/Cultivation in Schneider's), agile beliefs will be much more easily accepted and agile has a greater chance of leading to emergent outcomes. If the culture is non-agile, prepare for the cultural shifts to come.

5. Reiterate and model beliefs that lead to agile values.

6. Culture change takes patience and time and leadership buy-in. When considering culture change, consider an agile approach:

- What incremental steps can be taken towards an agile culture?
- What examples could illustrate the importance of culture change to executives?
- Are there ways to test and demonstrate agile using small groups or pilots? What could succeed or fail quickly?

7.4 Coda and kudos

Over the past several years, Dave Thomas, Mike Cottmeyer, Stephen Cohen, Robert Galen, Tobias Mayer, Tim Ottinger, and others have all asked a similar question: "Is agile dead?" This led us to the theme of this book, that many view agile as a process rather than a change in values or a change in culture, especially those who might be later adopters or new to agile.

If agile is about changing culture, what does this culture look like? What are its values? Similarly, what are the values and beliefs of non-agilists?

Yves Hanoulle, Dan Rawsthorne, Ashish Pathak, Sebastian Sanitz, Pierre Neis, Ewan O'Leary, John Miller, Mark Levison, and Fred Brooks provided some of the early thoughts and questions that shaped this book in the online discussion "What beliefs do non-agilists share?"

This book might not be a surprise to those within the agile community. By describing end-goal agile values and illustrating with a variety of examples from different situations and businesses, we hope it both rekindles some of the original fire and helps bridge the gap with those newer to agile.

We'd like to thank Richard Kasperowski, Steve Bell, Eric Loder, and Ryan Meyer for reviewing early drafts; our significant others, Diane Hsiung and Theresa Kramer, for putting up with us and all of their support; Mollie Brumm and Laurie Nyveen, our copy editors, for making sure everything is succinct, clear, and grammatically correct; and Maiez Mehdi for his beautiful cover design. We'd also like to thank Ana Ciobotaru and Shane Hastie at InfoQ for all their help, encouragement, and support.

Figure 7.2: Collecting arrows and scoring at the Dunster archery competition, Somerset [IDS09].

Here, we've shared our perspective about why Agile works for complex development: it starts with beliefs that reinforce or lead to certain core values. We've described the most crucial values to bring them to the surface and highlight the end goal of transformation. We've found it helps to see what these values look like in practice and how Agile Manifesto beliefs can lead to the organizational values of trust, responsibility, learning, and collaboration. The simple idea is that if you can see the target, it's easier to hit.

If something works wonderfully for you or you learned something new, please write. If something didn't work or you have a different perspective, please write.

We look forward to hearing from you and hope to find new tales of failure and success.

— Michael and David

Michael de la Maza is an agile consultant and angel investor. As an agile consultant, his major engagements have been with PayPal, State Street, edX, Carbonite, Unum, and Symantec. Previously, he was VP of corporate strategy at Softricity (acquired by Microsoft in 2006) and co-founder of Inquira (acquired by Oracle in 2011). He holds a Ph.D. in computer science from MIT and is a Certified Enterprise Coach (CEC), formerly known as a Certified Scrum Coach (CSC). He can be reached at michael.delamaza@gmail.com.

David Benz is an instructional designer, trainer, and computer engineer who has designed award-winning training for Cisco Systems, Convergys, Luxottica, Apple, Great American Insurance, and Marsh & McLennan Companies. He develops classes in negotiation, influencing without authority, solution selling, organizational change, and leadership, and can be reached at davidbenz@fuse.net.

ADDITIONAL RESOURCES

This book focused on agile as a framework for change and the subsequent culture that agile beliefs have the potential to create.

Other resources for helping organizations transform include:

- *Coaching Agile Teams: A Companion for ScrumMasters, Agile Coaches, and Project Managers in Transition* by Lyssa Adkins.
- *The Culture Game: Tools for the Agile Manager* by Daniel Mezick.
- *The Leader's Guide to Radical Management* and *The Leader's Guide to Storytelling* by Stephen Denning.
- *Leading Change* by John Kotter.
- *30 Days to Better Agile: Effective Strategies for Getting Results Fast Using Scrum* by Angela Druckman.
- *Overcoming Organizational Defenses* by Chris Argyris.
- *The Agile Mindset: The Thinking That Makes Agile Processes Work* by Gil Broza.
- *Reframing Organizations: Artistry, Choice, and Leadership* by Lee G. Bolman and Terrence E. Deal.
- *Drive: The Surprising Truth About What Motivates Us* by Daniel Pink.
- *Software for Your Head: Core Protocols for Creating and Maintaining Shared Vision* by Jim and Michele McCarthy.
- *Lean Change Management: Innovative Practices for Managing Organizational Change* by Jason Little

Questions about organizational values

The agile values framework can be used as a guide to help organizations understand the culture they want to achieve.

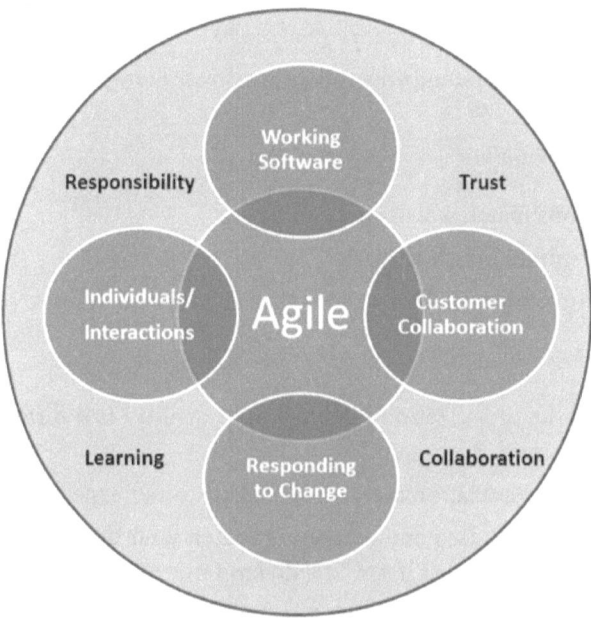

The agile values framework.

Trust	Responsibility	Learning	Collaboration
Openness	Autonomy/ Freedom	Risk	Transparency
Credibility/ Integrity	Motivation	Feedback	Self-organization
Craftsman-ship	Commitment	Adaptabil-ity	Communication
Empathy/ Respect	Mutual Responsibility	Sharing	Unity/ Shared Purpose

Aspects of agile values.

You can use the following list of questions from the chapters and sub-chapters on values to evaluate the culture of an organization.

Trust

Openness

- Do you hear the bad as well as the good?
- Are issues raised or hidden?
- Do people understand why things are done? How transparent are decisions?

Integrity and credibility

- Do actions match words?
- Do incentives match rhetoric?
- Are people rewarded for actions that demonstrate values?

Craftsmanship

- What is the organization's definition of quality? Is it different internally than with customers?
- Does the organization meet or exceed customer expectations?
- Does your branding and marketing match your delivery? Does your organization do what it says it'll do (and more)?
- How do coworkers learn about each other's skills and results within the organization?
- What's the relationship between sales and delivery?

Empathy and respect

- How is respect observed within the organization? What examples of respect and empathy can you cite?
- How are differences viewed within the organization?
- Are people more inward-focused or outward-focused? Do they lean towards thinking about others or their own self-preservation?
- What characteristics are respected within the organization?

Responsibility

Autonomy and freedom

- At what level are people free to make decisions? What types of decisions?

- When goals are established, are teams free to determine how to get there?
- How are goals communicated within the organization? Who is responsible?
- Are teams responsible for how goals are achieved?

Motivation

- Do teams and individuals understand why the organization does what it does?
- Do individuals understand why their group does what it does and how this relates to the overall mission of the organization?
- Does the mission fit in with ideas about how to make the world better?

Commitment

- What types of commitments do teams and individuals make? How?
- Do people on the team know who is responsible for what?

Mutual responsibility

- Do people accept responsibility for their actions?
- Do people respond defensively or feel threatened?
- When issues are encountered, how does the team react? Do they work together to solve challenges? Or do they place blame?
- Do people feel responsible for others on the team?

Learning

Risk

- Are people encouraged to seek out new ideas and try new things?
- How does the organization define innovation? How do leaders view mistakes and risk?
- What happens when people make mistakes? Are they shut down when something doesn't work? Is it safe within the culture to take risks?
- How does the organization provide new opportunities and challenges?

Feedback

- What mechanisms exist to provide feedback?
- How do people know when something isn't working?
- What types of feedback are acted on and how?
- How easy is it in the organization to ask questions and receive honest answers?

Adaptability

- Are disruptive technologies recognized?
- How difficult is it to take a different direction? (This could be targeting a different market, looking at new technology that might hurt your current business, or examining the ways you do business in light of new trends and disruptions.)
- At what rate is your organization improving? (If the rate is not greater than your competitors, all it does is delay your demise.)
- What happens when someone suggests a different approach in response to changing conditions?

Sharing

- Where is knowledge created and located?
- How are best practices captured, shared, and adopted?
- How does the organization encourage individual development? Team development?
- What divides exist within the organization and how is communication established between these divides?
- Are teams and individuals rewarded for sharing?
- Are agile teams becoming inbred so that they can't share across teams and/or functions? How often do great ideas "hop ponds"?

Collaboration

Transparency

- How does the organization address impediments within teams? Across teams?
- Is there a common etiquette within the organization and does this etiquette allow for transparent communication?

- At what level are development teams involved in business decisions? Or internal business organizations with development?

Self-organization

- How do people organize and work implicitly? Are they handing off work or are they doing work together?
- Are talents understood within groups, and do people seek out experts?
- Do teams have access to resources as needed?
- What level of decision making are teams responsible for?
- What is the perception of what a team is and how it functions? Is teamwork perceived as being nice to one another?

Communication

- How does knowledge circulate within the organization? Within teams? Among teams?
- How do people within and outside the group communicate?
- When someone needs something, how soon do they ask?
- How is feedback provided (on projects, on and to managers, to employees)?
- Can people joke with each other? Are people laughing and having fun? (Humor typically relies on shared values. When you hear people joking with each other, it's a sign that they know and trust each other.)

Unity and shared purpose

- What processes are in place to create competition and do they have unintended consequences?
- If you asked 10 people from different groups, would each tell you a similar story about the goal of the organization?

REFERENCES

References

[Act86] "Act for Establishing Religious Freedom, January, 16, 1786." Virginia MemoRy: Library of Virginia. http://www.virginia-memory.com/online_classroom/shaping_the_constitution/doc/religious_freedom.

[Adk10] Adkins, Lyssa. Coaching Agile Teams: A Companion for ScrumMasters, Agile Coaches, and Project Managers in Transition. Addison-Wesley Professional, Boston, MA, 2010.

[All14] Allain, Rhett. "Two Common Misconceptions About Learning." Wired. Sept. 1, 2014. http://www.wired.com/2014/09/two-common-misconceptions-about-learning/.

[Ama13] Amann, Wolfgang and Stachowicz-Stanusch, Agata. Integrity in Organizations: Building the Foundations for Humanistic Management. Palgrave Macmillan. New York, NY, 2013.

[ANTA15] "Values Statement - Enron." Australian National Training Authority. https://www.dlsweb.rmit.edu.au/toolbox/knowmang/content/ethics/values_statement_enron.htm.

[Ant15] The Anti-Agile Manifesto. 2015. http://antiagilemanifesto.com/.

[Arg90] Argyris, Chris. Overcoming Organizational Defenses: Facilitating Organizational Learning. Needham Heights, MA: Allyn & Bacon, 1990.

[Arg98] Argyris, Chris. "Empowerment: The Emperor's New Clothes." Harvard Business Review. May-June 1998. p. 98-105.

[Ash15] Ashkenas, Ron. "There's a Difference Between Cooperation and Collaboration." Harvard Business Review. April 20, 2015. https://hbr.org/2015/04/theres-a-difference-between-cooperation-and-collaboration.

[Asp04] Asproni, Giovanni. "Motivation, Teamwork, and Agile Development." Agile

Times. Vol. 4, February 2004. http://teambuildingtools.wikispaces.umb.edu/file/view/Motivation+Teamwork+and+Agile+Development.pdf.

[Bee09] Beerel, Annabel. Leadership and Change Management. London: SAGE Publications Ltd., 2009.

[Bol97] Bolman, Lee and Deal, Terrence. Reframing Organizations: Artistry, Choice, and Leadership. San Francisco, CA:

Jossey-Bass, 1997.

[Bro15] Broza, Gil. The Agile Mindset: The Thinking That Makes Agile Processes Work. LeanPub, 2015. http://www.leanpub.com/theagilemindset/.

[Bur07] Burgess, Paul. Natural Born Success: Discover the Instinctive Drives That Make You Tick! Sydney: Wrightbooks, 2007. http://instinctivedrives.com/.

[Car15] Carmichael, Lindsey E. Forensic Science: In Pursuit of Justice. Minneapolis, Minnesota: Essential Library, 2015.

[Cha08] Chapman, Geoffrey. "A canonical correlation analysis of the Myers-Briggs type indicator and the Instinctive Drives system." 2008 Conference of the Australia and New Zealand Academy of Management. New Zealand: University of Auckland, 2008.

[Chr97] Christensen, Clayton M. The Innovator's Dilemma: When New Technologies Cause Great Firms to Fail. Boston, MA: Harvard Business School Press, 1997.

[Cis14] Cisco Japan PR. "Cisco Nexus 9000 Series Family." Cisco Systems, 2014. https://www.flickr.com/photos/ciscojapan-pr/13836984983.

[Cis15] Cisco Systems. "Transforming Collaboration Through Strategy and Architecture." Cisco Systems Whitepaper, 2015. https://www.cisco.com/en/US/services/ps2961/ps2664/Trans-forming_Collaboration_through_Strategy_Architecture.pdf.

[Coa60] Coase, R.H. "The problem of social cost." The Journal of Law & Economics. Vol III, October, 1960.

[Coh11] Cohen, Stephen. "Has Agile Jumped the Shark?" MSDN Blogs. May 11, 2011. http://blogs.msdn.com/b/stephen_cohen/archive/2011/05/02/has-agile-has-jumped-the-shark.aspx.

[Con11] Connors, Roger and Smith, Tom. Change the Culture, Change the Game: The Breakthrough Strategy for Energizing Your Organization and Creating Accountability for Results. New York: Portfolio Penguin, 2011.

[Cos10] Costello, Amy. "Southern Africa: Troubled Water." Frontline World. June 29, 2010. http://www.pbs.org/frontline-world/stories/southernafrica904/video_index.html.

[Cot11] Cottmeyer, Mike. "Untangling Adoption and Transformation." Leading Agile. January 13, 2011. http://www.leadingagile.com/2011/01/untangling-adoption-and-transformation/.

[Cov06] Covey, Stephen M.R. The Speed of Trust: The One Thing That Changes Everything. New York: Free Press, 2006.

[Dec85] Deci, Edward L. and Ryan, Richard M. Intrinsic Motivation and Self-determination in Human Behavior. New York: Plenum Press, 1985.

[Dee11] Deepwater Horizon Study Group. "Final Report on the Investigation of the MacondoWell Blowout." DHSG. March 1, 2011. http://ccrm.berkeley.edu/pdfs_papers/bea_pdfs/dhsgfinal-report-march2011-tag.pdf.

[Del15] de la Maza, Michael. "What beliefs do non-agilists share?" Google Groups- Scrum Alliance Forum. March 2, 2015. https://groups.google.com/forum/#!topic/scrumalliance/9r6knBffJal.

[Den10] Denning, Stephen. The Leader's Guide to Radical Management. San Francisco: Jossey-Bass, 2011.

[Den15] Denning, Stephen. "How to make the whole organization Agile." Forbes.

http://www.forbes.com/sites/stevedenning/2015/07/22/how-to-make-the-whole-organization-agile/.

[Dun14] Duncan, Roger Dean. "Culture at Work: The Tyranny of Unwritten Rules." Forbes. February 13, 2014. http://www.forbes.com/sites/rodgerdeanduncan/2014/02/13/culture-at-work-the-tyranny-of-unwritten-rules/.

[Dutra11] Dutra, Ana. "Agile leaders—what do they look like?" Forbes. April 21, 2011. http://www.forbes.com/sites/anadutra/2011/04/21/agile-leaders-what-do-they-look-like/.

[Dys12] Dysart, Katie L. "Managing the CSI Effect in Jurors." American Bar Association May 28, 2012. http://apps.americanbar.org/litigation/committees/trialevidence/articles/winter-spring2012-0512-csieffect-jurors.html.

[Eld12] Elders, Tom. "I can't take this Agile crap any longer." Hacker News, 2012. https://news.ycombinator.com/

item?id=5406384.

[For21] Forbes, B.C. "Why Do So Many Men Never Amount to Anything?" Thomas A. Edison, the great inventor, answers this pointed question." American Magazine. January 1921.

[For09] Foremski, Tom. "Google Quietly Drops Its 'Don't Be Evil' Motto." Silicon Valley Watcher. April 1, 2009. http://www.silicon-valleywatcher.com/mt/archives/2009/04/google_quietly.php.

[For05] Forrester Consulting. "Unified Communications Transform Business Communication." 2005.

[For09] Fortnow, Lance. "The Status of the P Versus NP Problem." Communications of the ACM. Vol. 52 No. 9, 2009. p. 78-86.

[Fow01] Fowler, Martin et al. The Agile Manifesto. 2001. http://agilemanifesto.org.

[Gal14] Galen, Robert. "Has Agile Jumped the Shark? Part Deux!" RGalen Consulting. November 24, 2014. http://rgalen.com/agile-training-news/2014/11/17/has-agile-jumped-the-shark-part-deux.

[Gil13] Gill, Stephen J. "Future of Employee Learning." The Performance Improvement Blog. April 18, 2013. http:/stephen-jgill.typepad.com/performance_improvement_b/2013/04/future-of-employee-learning.html.

[Gla08] Glazer, Hillel et al. "CMI or Agile: Why Not Embrace Both!" The Software Engineering Institute. Carnegie-Mellon, 2008. http://resources.sei.cmu.edu/asset_files/Technical-Note/2008_004_001_14924.pdf.

[Han89] Handford, Thomas W. Andersen's Fairy Tales. New York: Belford, Clarke & Company, 1889.

[Han09] Hansen, Morton T. Collaboration: How Leaders Avoid the Traps, Create Unity, and Reap Big Results. Boston: Harvard Business School Publishing, 2009.

[Har11] Harford, Tim. Why Success Always Starts with Failure. New York: Farrar, Strauss, and Giroux, 2011.

[Har50] Harlow, Harry F., Harlow, Margaret Kuenne, and Meyer, Donald R. "Learning Motivated by a Manipulation Drive." Journal of Experimental Psychology. Vol 40(2), April 1950, p. 228-234.

[Hea07] Heath, Dan and Heath, Chip. Made to Stick: Why Some Ideas Survive and Others Die. New York: Random House, 2007.

[Heu10] Heusser, Jeff. "John Lasseter and Ed Catmull." Wikimedia.org. 2010. https://commons.wikimedia.org/wiki/File:VES_Awards_89.jpg.

[IDS09] IDS Photos. "Time to score, collecting arrows and scoring at Dunster Archery competition, Somerset, 2009." June 14, 2009.

[IBM15] "Our Values at Work." IBM. http://www.ibm.com/ibm/values/us/.

[Jet15] "Corporate and Social Responsibility." jetBlue. https://www.jetblue.com/corporate-social-responsibility/.

[Jon06] Jones, Del. "CEOs say how you treat a waiter can predict a lot about character." USA Today. April 17, 2006. http://usatoday30.usatoday.com/money/companies/management/2006-04-14-ceos-waiter-rule_x.htm.

[Kim13] Kimes, Mina. "At Sears, Eddie Lampert's Warring Divisions Model Adds to the Troubles" Bloomberg. July 11, 2013. http://www.bloomberg.com/bw/articles/2013-07-11/at-sears-eddie-lamperts-warring-divisionsmodel-adds-to-the-troubles.

[Kni13] Kniberg, Henrik. "Culture Over Process." Launchpad, Bangkok. December 18, 2013. https://www.youtube.com/watch?v=Rb0O0Lgs9zU.

[Kot96] Kotter, John. Leading Change. Boston: Harvard Business School Press, 1996.

[Kot11] Kotter, John. "Change Management vs. Change Leadership." Forbes July 12, 2011. http://www.forbes.com/sites/johnkotter/2011/07/12/change-management-vs-change-leadership-whats-the-difference/.

[Kra13] Krakovsky, Marina. "Charles O'Reilly: Why Some Companies Seem to Last Forever." Insights by Stanford Business. May 31, 2013. https://www.gsb.stanford.edu/insights/charles-oreilly-why-some-companies-seem-last-forever.

[Kru99] Kruger, Justin and Dunning, David. "Unskilled and Unaware of It: How Difficulties in Recognizing One's Own Incompetence Lead to Inflated Self-Assessments." Journal of Personality and Social Psychology. Vol 77, No. 6, 1999. p. 1121-1134.

http://psych.colorado.edu/vanboven/teaching/p7536_heurbias/p7536_readings/kruger_dunning.pdf.

[Kun02] Kunen, James. "Enron's Vision (and Values) Thing." New York Times. January 19, 2002. http://www.nytimes.com/2002/01/19/opinion/enron-s-vision-and-values-thing.html.

[Lal14] Laloux, Fredric. Reinventing Organizations Brussels: Nelson Parker, 2014.

[Mak14] Makabee, Hayim. "The End of Agile: Death by Over-simplification." Effective Software Design. March 17, 2014. http://effectivesoftwaredesign.com/2014/03/17/the-end-of-agile-death-by-over-simplification/.

[Man15] Mancuso, Sandra. The Software Craftsman: Professionalism, Pragmatism, Pride. Upper Saddle River, NJ: Prentice-Hall, 2015.

[Mas43] Maslow, A.H. "A Theory of Human Motivation." Psychological Review. Vol 50, 1943. p. 370-396. http://psychclassics.yorku.ca/Maslow/motivation.htm.

[May13] Mayer, Tobias. The People's Scrum: Agile Ideas for Revolutionary Transformation. San Francisco: Dymaxicon, 2013.

[McC02] McCarthy, Jim and Michele. Software for Your Head: Core Protocols for Creating and Maintaining Shared Vision. New York: Addison-Wesley, 2002.

[McG60] McGregor, Douglas. The Human Side of Enterprise. New York: McGraw-Hill, 1960.

[McK09] McKnight, Michelynn. The Agile Librarian's Guide to Thriving in Any Institution. Santa Barbara: Libraries Unlimited, 2009.

[McL13] McLaughlin, Kevin. "The Super-Secret Startup That's Going to Save Cisco Just Had Its Coming Out Party (Sort Of)." Business Insider. June 26, 2013. http://www.businessinsider.com/cisco-shares-some-detailsabout-insieme-2013-6.

[Mic15] Michael, Jonathan. "The Pixar Way: 37 Quotes on Developing and Maintaining a Creative Company." Bplans.com. http://articles.bplans.com/

[Mil14] Miller, Laurie. "2014 State of the Industry Report: Spending on Employee Training Remains a Priority." Training + Development Magazine. November 8, 2014. https://www.td.org/

Publications/Magazines/TD/TD-Archive/2014/11/2014-State-of-the-Industry-Report-Spending-on-Employee-Training-Remains-a-Priority.

[Mil11] Milway, Katie Smith and Saxton, Amy. "The Challenge of Organizational Learning." Stanford Social Innovation Review. Summer 2011. http://www.ssireview.org/articles/entry/the_challenge_of_organizational_learning.

[Mon13] Monsen, Karen and de Blok, Jos. "Buurtzorg, Nederland." American Journal of Nurses. August 2013, p. 55-59. http://buurtzorgusa.org/PDF/AJN.pdf.

[Mor06] Morris, Scott. "The waiter rule." 2006. Reprinted with permission of the artist.

[NOS12] National Ocean Service. "Iceberg." National Oceanic and Atmospheric Administration. 2012. https://www.flickr.com/photos/usoceangov/8290528771.

[Nor15] Nordstrom. "Nordstrom Company History." http://shop.nordstrom.com/c/company-history.

[Off15] OfficeSnapShots.com. "Smart, New, Agile, and Activity-Based: Six Examples of Your Future Office." 2015. http://officesnapshots.com/articles/smart-new-agile-and-activity-based-working-six-examples-of-yourfuture-office-design/.

[Ott14] Ottinger, Tim. "I want Agile back." AgileOtter.com. February 12, 2014. http://agileotter.blogspot.com/2014/02/i-want-agile-back.html.

[Pat15] Patagonia. "Patagonia's Mission Statement." http://www.patagonia.com/us/patagonia.go?assetid=2047.

[Pie11] Pietri,William. "Agile's Second Chasm (and how we fell in)." Agile Focus. February 21, 2011. http://agilefocus.com/2011/02/21/agiles-second-chasm-and-how-we-fell-in/.

[Pin09] Pink, Daniel. "The puzzle of motivation." TEDGlobal 2009. July, 2009. http://www.ted.com/talks/dan_pink_on_motivation.

[Pin09] Pink, Daniel. Drive: The Surprising Truth About What Motivates Us. New York: Riverhead Books, 2009.

[Pix14] Pixton, Pollyanna et al. The Agile Culture: Leading through Trust and Ownership. 2014. Boston: Addison-Wesley Professional, 2014.

[Put14] Putnam-Delaney, Keith. "Tech's best-kept secret: How agile development can be a game-changer for SMBs." Dropbox for Business. November 17, 2014. https://blogs.dropbox.com/business/2014/11/agile-development-forsmbs/

[Pyr03] Pyritz, Bill. "Craftsmanship versus engineering: Computer programming - An art or a science?" Bell Labs Technical Journal. Volume 8, Issue 3. Fall 2003.

[Reh14] Rehm, Diane. "Ed Catmull: Creativity, Inc.: Overcoming the Unseen Forces that Stand in the way of True Inspiration." The Diane Rehm Show. May 5, 2014. http://thedianerehmshow.org/shows/2014-05-05/ed-catmullcreativity-inc-overcoming-unseen-forces-stand-way-true-inspiration.

[Sah04] Sahota, Michael. "How to Make Your Culture Work with Agile, Kanban & Software Craftsmanship." Methods & Tools. Winter 2011. http://www.methodsandtools.com/archive/agileculture.php.

[Sar04] Saran, Cliff. "European banking giant adopts agile development methodology." Computer Weekly. November 2004. http://www.computerweekly.com/feature/European-banking-giant-adopts-agile-development-methodology.

[Sch94] Schneider, William. The Reengineering Alternative: A Plan for Making Your Current Culture Work. New York: Irwin Professional Publishing, 1994.

[Sco09] Scott, Owen. "The PlayPump." A series of blog posts. 2009. http://thoughtsfrommalawi.blogspot.com/2009/10/playpump-ii.html.

[Ser14] Serwer, Andy and Chambers, John. "How It All Connects." Fortune Brainstorm Tech. July 15, 2014. https://www.youtube.com/watch?v=0yDRt-IPkEM.

[Sha00] Shattuck, Lawrence G. "Communicating Intent and Imparting Presence." Military Review. March-April 2000. p. 66-72.

[She56] Sherif, Muzafer. "The Robber's Cave: Experiments in group conflict." Scientific American. Vol. 195, No. 5, 1956. p. 59-64.

[She61] Sherif, Muzafer. Intergroup Conflict and Cooperation: The Robbers Cave Experiment. Oklahoma: The University of Oklamahoma, 1961.

[Sim11] Simmons, Bret. "Leadership Done Right: Example from

'We Were Soldiers'." Positive Organizational Behavior. Apr. 30, 2011. https://www.youtube.com/watch?v=p3Y_A5Mz7jA.

[Sin09] Sinek, Simon. "How great leaders inspire action." TED. Sep, 2009. http://www.ted.com/talks/simon_sinek_how_great_leaders_inspire_action?language=en.

[Sin14] Sinek, Simon. Leaders Eat Last: Why Some Teams Pull Together and Others Don't. New York: Penguin, 2014.

[Sin12] Singleton, Andy. "Seven Things I Hate About Agile." Assembla. August 22, 2012. http://blog.assembla.com/AssemblaBlog/tabid/12618/bid/87899/Seven-Things-I-Hate-About-Agile.aspx.

[Smi88] Smith, Douglas K. and Alexander, Robert C. Fumbling the Future: How Xerox Invented, Then Ignored, the First Personal Computer. New York: W. Morrow, 1988.

[Smi04] Smith, Douglas K. On Value and Values. Upper Saddle River, NJ: FT Press, 2004.

[Spa10] Spayd, Michael. "Agile & Culture: The Results." Collective Edge Coaching. July 6, 2010. http://collectiveedgecoaching.com/2010/07/agile_culture/.

[Str09] Strode, Diane E. et al. "The Impact of Organizational Culture on Agile Method Use." Proceedings of the 42nd Hawaii International Conference on System Sciences. 2009.

[Sur04] Surowiecki, James. The Wisdom of Crowds. New York: Doubleday, 2004.

[Sut14] Sutherland, Jeff. Scrum: The Art of Doing Twice the Work in Half the Time. New York: Crown Business, 2014.

[Tab06] Tabaka, Jean. Collaboration Explained: Facilitation Skills for Software Project Leaders. New York: Addison-Wesley Professional, 2006.

[Tai05] Tai, Kaihsu. "Steven Koonin, BP's then-Chief Scientist, speaking in the company boardroom in 2005." 2005. https://en.wikipedia.org/wiki/BP#/media/File:Steven_Koonin_BP_2005-02-22.jpg.

[Tai10] Taibbi, Matt. "The Great American Bubble Machine." Rolling Stone. April 10, 2010.

[Tat13] Tate, Ryan. "Google Couldn't Kill 20 Percent Time Even if it Wanted to." Wired. October 8, 2013. http://www.wired.

com/2013/08/20-percent-timewill-never-die/.

[Tet06] Tetlock, Philip. Expert Political Judgment: How Good Is It? How Can We Know? New Haven, CT: Princeton University Press, 2006.

[Tho14] Thomas, Dave. "Agile is Dead." PragDave. March 4, 2014. http://pragdave.me/blog/2014/03/04/time-to-kill-agile/.

[Tig09] Tighe, Mark. "Kodak DC220 Camera." 2007. https://commons.wikimedia.org/wiki/File:Kodak_DC220_zoom_front.jpg.

[Tuf09] Tufte, Edward. The Cognitive Style of PowerPoint. Aug. 6, 2012. http://users.ha.uth.gr/tgd/pt0501/09/Tufte.pdf.

[Tur05] Turknett, Robert and Cathy. "Respect - The Will to Understand." Northern Illinois University. 2005. http://www.niu.edu/hrs/work_life/employee_assistance/resources/downloads/Coashing%20-%20Respect%20Handout.pdf.

[Ver14] VersionOne. "2014 State of Agile." March 26, 2015. http://www.versionone.com/about-us/press-releases/article/VersionOne-Releases-9th-Annual-State-of-Agile-Survey-Results/.

[Zap15] Zappos.com. "About Zappos Culture." http://www.zappos.com/d/about-zappos-culture.

INDEX

Toy Story, 113
2014 State of Agile survey, 7, 8
2014 State of Talent Development report, 93
80/20 rule, 89, 90

adaptability, 77, 85–88, 129, 132
Adkins, Lyssa, 99, 119, 128
Agile
    adoption, 7–10
    Adoption Framework, 4
    beliefs, 6, 21-24, 35, 36, 76, 80, 81, 88, 118, 119
    culture, 118–122
    framework for change, 6, 24, 30, 120
    Journey Index, 4
    leaders, 3
    Manifesto, 4, 6, 21, 22, 28, 84, 85,100, 104, 120, 123
    principles, 22, 35, 36, 54, 60, 64, 100, 107
    self-organizing teams, 67-69, 96, 101, 104-106
    transformation, 7–10, 26-30, 119
    values, 26–30, 118–122, 129
    values framework, 26–30, 129–133
        aspects, 29, 129-133
AgilityHealth, 4
Alexander, Robert, 87
Andersen, Hans Christian, 101, 102
Andiamo Systems, 80
Anti-Agile Manifesto, 4
Apple, 62, 63, 87, 89
Argyris, Chris, 66-68, 102, 128
AskKenas, Ron, 98
Auftragstaktik, 59
autonomy, 58-60, 129-131

beliefs, 12–24
BNP Paribas, 3
Bolman, Lee G., 128
British Petroleum (BP), 20, 21
Broza, Gil, 2, 128
Bush, George W., 74
Bush, Laura, 81
business transformation, 41-43

Buurtzorg Nederland, 104–106

Cafiero, Luca, 80
Cagley, Meghan, 68
Cagley, Thomas, 68
Capability Maturity Model (CMM), 2
Capability Maturity Model Integration (CMMI), 2
Case, Steve, 81
Catalyst Switches, 79, 80
Catmull, Ed, 12, 113–115
Certified Agile Tester (CAT), 4
Chambers, John, 80
Chapman, Geoffrey, 66
Christensen, Clayton, 87
Cisco Systems, 41-43, 64, 79, 80
Clay Mathematics Institute (CMI), 75
co-locating teams, 108, 109
Coase, Ronald, 100
Cohen, Stephen, 4, 122
collaboration, 10, 29, 95–115, 129, 132, 133
    aspects, 101
    beliefs that undermine collaboration,112, 113
    beliefs to emphasize, 112
    communication, 101, 106–109, 129, 133
    self-organization, 101, 104–106, 129,133
    shared purpose, 101, 109–111, 129,133
    transparency, 101–104, 129, 132, 133
    unity, 101, 109–111, 129, 133
Collective Edge Coaching, 96
commander's intent, 59, 60
commitment, 59, 66–68, 129, 131
    external, 67, 68
    internal, 67, 68
communication, 101, 106–109, 129, 133
Comparative Agility, 4
Connors, Roger, 16
cooperation, 32, 97–99
Core Protocols, 90-92
Cottmeyer, Mike, 8, 119
Covey, Stephen M.R., 34, 45
craftsmanship, 36, 37, 43–45, 129, 130

credibility, 36, 37, 40–43, 129, 130
Crescendo Communications, 79
crossing the chasm, 4–7
CSI effect, 75
culture, 16-20, 118-122

Dalio, Ray, 103
de Blok, Jos, 104-106
Deal, Terrence E., 128
Deci, Edward, 61
Denning, Stephen, 121, 128
design by committee, 97–99
disruptive technologies, 87, 88, 132
Druckman, Angela, 128
Dunning, David, 83
Dunning-Kruger effect, 83–85
Dynamic Systems Development Method (DSDM), 4

Edison, Thomas, 78, 79
Elders, Tom, 4
empathy, 36, 37, 45-48, 129, 130
Enron, 35, 40
evidence-based management, 4
evolution of organizations, 24–27, 29, 96, 97
    amber, 24–27, 96
    green, 24–27, 96
    magenta, 24
    orange, 24–27, 96
    red, 24–27, 96
    teal, 24–27, 96
extrinsic motivation, 62

feedback, 77, 81–85, 129, 132
Fibre channel storage, 80
Forrester, 4
freedom, 58-60, 129-131

Galen, Robert, 4, 122
Galloway, Joe, 69
Gerstner Jr., Louis, 106, 107
Gibson, Paul, 54

Google, 20
Google 20% time, 93

handoff time, 108, 109
Hansen, Morten, 111
Harlow, Harry, 61
Horn Interactive, 50–52

IBM, 20, 88, 106, 107
inauthentic behavior, 101, 102
individual values, 12, 13, 19, 27
InfoQ, 5
innovator's dilemma, 87
Insieme, 79, 80
Instinctive Drives™, 64–66
integrity, 36, 37, 40–43, 129, 130
International Software Testing Qualifications Board (ISTQB), 4
intrinsic motivation, 61
IP telephony, 41

Jain, Prem, 80
Jay-Z, 81
Jefferson, Thomas, 14-16
jetBlue, 20
Johnson & Johnson, 88

Kanban, 3, 30, 120
Kerry, John, 74
Kniberg, Henrik, 7, 8, 118, 119
Knowledge Is Power Program, 90
Kodak, 86
Kolditz, Tom, 60
Kotter, John, 128
Kruger, Justin, 83
Kunen, James, 40

Laloux, Fredric, 10, 24-27 96, 122
Lampert, Eddie, 109, 110
LeanKanBan University, 3
learning, 10, 29, 73–94, 129, 131, 132

adaptability, 77, 85–88, 125, 132
aspects, 77
beliefs that undermine learning, 92, 93
beliefs to emphasize, 92
feedback, 77, 81–85, 129, 132
risk, 77–81, 129, 131
sharing, 77, 89–92, 125, 132
Little, Jason, 128

Makabee, Hayim, 4
Mancuso, Sandro, 43
Marquis, Josh, 75
Maslow's hierarchy of needs, 33
Maslow, Abraham, 33
mastery, 62, 111
Mayer, Tobias, 6,120
Mazzola, Mario, 80
McCarthy, Jim, 40, 90, 128
McCarthy, Michele, 40, 90, 128
McGregor, Douglas, 32-34, 50
Menlo Park, 78
Mezick, Dan, 19, 23, 128
Microsoft, 90, 93
Monsen, Karen, 105
Moore, Geoffrey, 4–7
Moore, Hal, 69
motivation, 58, 60–66, 129, 131
mutual responsibility, 58, 69, 70, 129, 131
Myers-Briggs, 66

National Public Radio (NPR), 3
Nexus 9000, 79, 80
Nickolaisen, Niel, 54
Nordstrom, 20
Nuova Systems, 80

O'Reilly, Charles, 88
Oakes, Kim, 90
openness, 36–39, 129, 130
organizational change, 6, 7, 10, 117-122
organizational culture, 7-10, 16-27, 118-122

organizational values, 8, 24-30, 118
  questions, 129–133
Ormerod, Paul, 74
Ottinger, Tim, 4, 122

P vs. NP problem, 75
Pagonis, Gus, 46
Palo Alto Research Center (PARC), 87
Patagonia, 20
Pecha Kucha, 38, 39
Photoshop wars, 51
Pietri, William, 6
Pink, Daniel, 62, 111, 128
Pixar Studios, 113–115
Pixton, Pollyanna, 54
PlayPumps, 81–83
PowerPoint, 107
prediction, 74-77
process change, 5, 18, 119-122
Project Management Institute (PMI), 3
purpose, 29, 60–64
Pyritz, Bill, 44, 45

radical transparency, 103, 104
recommendations for coaches, 122
recommendations for executives, 121, 122
Rehm, Diane, 113
respect, 36, 37, 45-48, 129, 130
responsibility, 10, 29, 53–72, 129-131
  aspects, 58
  autonomy, 58-60, 129-131
  beliefs that undermine responsibility, 71
  beliefs to emphasize, 70, 71
  commitment, 58, 66–68, 129, 131
  freedom, 58-60, 129-131
  motivation, 58, 60–66, 129, 131
  mutual responsibility, 58, 69, 70, 129, 131
Results Pyramid, 10, 16–19, 23
risk, 77–81, 129, 131
Robbers Cave Experiment, 110, 111

Roosevelt, Theodore, 2

SAFe, 4
Sahota, Michael, 9, 96
Sarbanes-Oxley, 35
Scaled Agile Framework(SAFe), 4
Schmidt, Jean, 74, 75
Schneider's cultural model, 96
Schneider, William, 96
Scott, Owen, 82
Scrum, 2-6, 28-30, 43, 68, 71, 103, 118–120
    code of ethics, 68
    values, 29
Scrum Alliance, 3, 29
Scrum.org, 3
SCRUMStudy, 4
Sears, 109, 110
self-organization, 101, 104–106, 129,133
Selsius Systems, 41
shared purpose, 101, 109–111, 129,133
sharing, 77, 89–92, 125, 132
Sherif, Muzafer, 110, 111
Shuhari, 119
Siebel, 8
Sinek, Simon, 62–64
Singleton, Andy, 4
Smith, Douglas K., 12, 87
Smith, Tom, 16
software-defined networking (SDN), 79, 80
Spayd, Michael, 96
spin-in, 79, 80
Spotify, 118, 119
state of Agile, 7-9
Surowiecki, James, 99
sustaining technologies, 87
Sutherland, Jeff, 29

Tabaka, Jean, 96, 97
Tetlock, Philip, 74, 77
Thatcher, Margaret, 75
Theory X, 32-34, 50

Theory Y, 32–34, 50
Thomas, Dave, 4, 7
Toyota, 88
transparency, 101–104, 129, 132, 133
trust, 10, 29, 31–52, 54–58, 129, 130
    aspects, 36, 37 129
    beliefs that undermine trust, 49, 50
    beliefs to emphasize, 49
    craftsmanship, 36, 37, 43–45, 129, 130
    credibility, 36, 37, 40–43, 129, 130
    empathy, 36, 37, 45-48, 129, 130
    integrity, 36, 37, 40–43, 129, 130
    openness, 36–39, 129, 130
    respect, 36, 37, 45-48, 129, 130
Tufte, Edward, 106
Tyco International, 35

Unified Communications, 41
Unified Computing System (UCS), 80
unity, 101, 109–111, 129, 133

values, 11–30
VersionOne, 7-9
Virginia Statute for Religious Freedom,
14
Voice over IP, 50

waiter rule, 47, 48
Walt Disney Studios, 114
WorldCom, 35

Xerox, 86, 87

Zappos, 20

www.ingramcontent.com/pod-product-compliance
Lightning Source LLC
Chambersburg PA
CBHW032024170526
45157CB00002B/846